MEET CHRIST AND LIVE!

Other works by Michel Quoist also
published by Gill and Macmillan

Prayers of Life
The Christian Response
Christ is Alive

MEET CHRIST AND LIVE!

MICHEL QUOIST

translated by
J. F. BERNARD

GILL AND MACMILLAN

First published in 1973
Gill and Macmillan Ltd
2 Belvedere Place
Dublin 1
and internationally through
association with the
Macmillan Publishers Group

Originally published in France by
Les Editions Ouvrières, Paris, under
the title *Jésus Christ m'a donné rendez-vous*,
© Michel Quoist 1972

Translation © Doubleday & Company Inc. 1973

7171 0667 5

Cover design by Cor Klaasen

Grateful acknowledgement is made for the inclusion of
extracts from *The Jerusalem Bible*, © Darton,
Longman & Todd Ltd and Doubleday & Company
Inc. 1966, 1967, 1968, which are used
by permission of the publishers.

Printed and bound in Great Britain
by Richard Clay (The Chaucer Press), Ltd
Bungay, Suffolk

Contents

Foreword

I've looked at the world again. I've looked at mankind, and, above all, I've looked at the young. Some people refuse to look at the young. They look away to avoid seeing them, and they stop their ears so as not to hear them. But I look at them, and I listen to them. I might even say that they are my teachers.

I can't deny that young people are sometimes violent, unfair and everything else that their elders say about them. But they have this virtue, that they are capable of going right to the heart of things. They are not concerned with circumlocutions and fine distinctions. Therefore, they force us to *see*. They shake us out of our habitual complacency and our self-satisfaction with a way of thinking and a life-style which we no longer question sufficiently.

There are many people engaged in studying the problems of the young. Sociologists and psychologists devote themselves to learned analysis, and they are right to do so. But, as a Christian, I believe not that we should ignore such necessary investigations, but that we should go beyond them; that we should study the questions that they raise in a different light—in the light of faith.

Personally, I have done and continue to do a great deal of travelling. I've seen and listened to thousands of young people, individually and collectively. I've met them in developed, over-developed and underdeveloped countries. I've seen them live; I've listened to them express themselves. I've watched their violent demonstrations and their battles in the streets. I've observed them wandering down the dead-end streets of drug addiction, sexual excess and blind violence. I've listened to their endless discussions about the building of a new society and of a new man. In the midst of these sounds, or of an uneasy and sometimes agonised silence, I've heard, and I hear still, a great cry. It seems to come from afar at first, then it grows louder and breaks upon one like a storm: the cry of a man being asphyxiated.

Many people can no longer breathe. Their sense of the infinite has been repressed. They are struggling for air. They hunger and thirst for a food and drink they do not know. When they find a spring, they throw themselves upon it; and when a wise man appears, a guru, they fall upon their knees before him. Some discover Jesus. Is he the real Jesus, this Jesus whom politicians and commercial interests are already beginning to claim as their own? I do not know. Is he a sign? Why not? Surely, the Holy Spirit has not lost his power to inspire. In any case, I know for certain that some young people have already found Jesus. And I know that many more are searching for him, and that *they all need him*. The popular underground poster which reads: WANTED: A MAN CALLED JESUS, is on target.

I've also watched Christian adults. I've observed the way in which they've developed. It goes something like this: At first, many Christians lived, as it were, in the sacristy of the church, and occupied themselves with parish work and parish organisations. At one point, their priests told them that they should go out into the world. There, they were as strangers; and so, they set about becoming men again so that they could learn to love more perfectly. They followed in the footsteps of Jesus Christ, the Son of God who became man to save all men. They discovered the world—the world which is progressing, and which often progressed without them in the past. They came to know men who were struggling; and they, in their turn, joined in the struggle, no longer merely at the side of other men, but *with* them. After a few years, they came to realise, with their brothers-in-arms, that it was not easy to build a just world, and that even where battles had been won and new structures set up, man remained discouragingly the same and continued to spread the infection of his alienating selfishness.

Some people became discouraged. They began to look back, to doubt the value of their struggle, and then to question it. 'These things', they told themselves, 'are not, after all, the essential ones.' And, with that thought in mind, they withdrew from the world towards God, to whom they thought they had been unfaithful. They moved back into their ghettoes and found 'refuge' in prayer. Their scruples, of course, were merely alibis for worn-out fighters. They hoped to find among their friends, or in the depths of their own hearts, an oasis of peace; and there, they thought, they would encounter an accommodating God who would apply balm to their wounds.

Other people, rather than becoming discouraged by difficulties, were stimulated by them and became obsessed with the idea of saving the world. They were possessed by a mysterious, blind violence and threw themselves, heart and soul, into the battle. And, in so doing, they turned their eyes away from God. At first, they told themselves: 'We'll find God later, after we've won.' But later, they concluded: 'This is man's affair. It has nothing to do with God.'

Still others have refused to leave the battlefield and their companion-in-arms. They have also refused to fight without the God who sent them, and without the Christ who preceded them. They know that it is together, and only together, that the whole victory will be won. Therefore, they struggle with all their might not to lose sight of Jesus Christ. They know that he is alive; that he is risen; that he is working at their side in the world and in the hearts of men. But it is hard to see Jesus when no one else sees him.

Thus, we believe that many young people, in the midst of their searchings and worryings, their errors and rebellions, are reaching out to a Christ whom they do not know and have never met. What we must do is to reveal to them Jesus Christ, who is living among them.

We think too that many Christians have finally discovered Jesus Christ in their lives and in their actions. But, as we said earlier, some of them lose contact with him and then withdraw timidly from the world. Others also lose sight of him, but shrug, and continue to do battle. Still others have held firm and remain in their Father's field, with their elder Brother who is before them in the breach. These latter are often tired and hungry, because man is not yet accustomed to living with Jesus in his whole life. In this respect, comparatively few priests have been of real help. They have not been trained to offer such help, as we have often written and said. And yet, this is at the heart of a priest's work.

Jesus, the real Jesus, is waiting for us in life; yet, we pass him by without seeing him. We must learn to meet him, to think with him, to speak with him, and to act with him. The world is filled with talk of revolution, but there is only one true Revolution: that which will make all things new, beginning with the heart of man, in the depths of himself which man himself cannot reach, and then extending to the least and the greatest of our economic, political and social structures until it affects the whole universe. This Revolution cannot be realised without man. It cannot be realised without God. But it can be realised only by man in Jesus Christ and with Jesus Christ. After all, Jesus came into the world, yesterday and today, for that single purpose.

We have always tried to help our brothers live with Jesus. Perhaps a quick look at our past books will help to make clear the purpose of the present work.

The theme of *Aimer ou le journal de Dany* and also of *With love, Anne Marie*[1] was that an adolescent does not become first an adult and then an adult Christian but should grow simultaneously as a human and as a Christian. That is, boys and girls should grow with Christ.

In *The Christian Response*, I stressed that if a man wants to develop at all levels, if he wants to live and to commit himself effectively, he must live this great adventure with Jesus and in Jesus.

Prayers of Life aimed at showing that to live our lives with Jesus presupposes that we are in constant conversation with him in our daily lives.

In *Christ is Alive* I tried to answer the questions: Why is Jesus Christ present in the world? How? In what respect is faith a commitment to live Jesus' mystery of Creation and redeeming Incarnation with him?

And in the series, *Visages du Christ*,[2] instances were given of how today men live with Jesus in all walks of life, in all circumstances, at all ages. This is the Community of Witnesses, the mystery of the living Christ.

Here, I would like to describe a few practical exercises in living with Christ. Each chapter of this book is composed of the description of an event or situation, of a few reflections in the light of faith, and, finally of a short prayer.

All examples are inadequate, and mine are no exception. They do not form a coherent whole, and they are not arranged according to any definite plan. I could as easily have chosen other events and situations, made other reflections, prayed other prayers. Perhaps the sole merit of those included in this book are that they are not exercises of the imagina-

1. Newman Press, New York 1968.
2. *Freedom to Starve* by Paul Gallet, Gill and Macmillan 1970 (Penguin edition 1972 in Pelican Latin American Library) is the first of this series to be available in English translation. Consisting of the letters and diary notes of a French missionary priest in poverty-stricken north-east Brazil, it tells how he spends himself in labouring for 'the revolution of love' among people almost defeated by the horrifying conditions of their daily life.

tion. I have always tried to avoid imagining life. They are all bits and pieces taken from real life.

It was not I alone who undertook the task of re-examining life in the light of faith so as to discover the presence of the risen Christ. I did so, sometimes with one other person, sometimes with a single household, sometimes with a whole group of Christians. The result is this book, in which I have set down some of the things we discovered together, and some of our prayers. Obviously, I have done some editing and I have rearranged the material so as to include reflections from various sessions under one heading when they apply to the subject under discussion.

Another weakness of these 'practical exercises' is that they are incomplete. It would have been impossible for me to include all the possible reactions of the people I've worked with, their experiences while searching for Jesus, their discoveries, their gradual recognition of the presence of Christ, the development of their insights and their attitudes. All I can do here is suggest a few paths for the reader to follow and to go beyond. That is what it is all about. The lives of individuals and of groups are not stereotyped. Every man is different; and when Jesus issues an invitation, it is a very personal invitation. In that sense, this book should be read— and then forgotten. If it can lead a few Christians to the spot where Jesus is waiting silently for them, at the centre of their lives; if it can help them to recognise Jesus; if it can inspire them to encounter him and join him in his work of saving 'the whole man and the whole of mankind', then I will be satisfied.

1. Loving one's brother today

Our group discussion on the obligation of loving our brothers, and on how to do so at the practical level, was based on the gospel of St Matthew and on the Last Judgement. A month earlier, we had chosen St Matthew's gospel as our subject for personal meditation. When we got together to discuss our individual thoughts, there was a heated discussion. We came to realise that some of us, despite our 'commitment', had never gone beyond a very limited concept of charity. We were all aware of the importance of being solicitous for our neighbour's welfare, of exercising care in our inter-personal relationships, of giving ourselves totally to others. The social dimension of charity, however, the love of others through organisations and movements, seemed to be beyond the competence of faith, although we were willing enough to take it into account in practice. We therefore listened as Jesus explained again, in today's terms, the unconditional commandment of love.

You must love your brothers. That is an absolute requirement of our religion. 'Master, which is the greatest commandment of the Law?' . . . 'You must love the Lord your God with all your heart, with all your soul, and with all your mind. This is the greatest and the first commandment. The second resembles it: You must love your neighbour as yourself' (*Matt.* 22: 36-40).

Jesus was not talking about advice, but about a commandment.

The love of our brothers is an infallible test of our love of

13

God. 'Anyone who says, "I love God," and hates his brother, is a liar, since a man who does not love the brother that he can see cannot love God, whom he has never seen' (1 *John* 4: 20).

To love our brothers does not mean that we must love them with our emotions, or that we must be 'sentimental' about them, for Jesus commands us to love even our enemies (*Matt.* 5: 44). To love our brothers means that we must wish for their true good, and that we must do all that we can with them to obtain that good. This requires an effort which presupposes total self-forgetfulness.

'This has taught us love—that he gave up his life for us; and we, too, ought to give up our lives for our brothers ... My children, our love is not to be just words or mere talk, but something real and active; only by this can we be certain that we are children of the truth' (1 *John* 3: 16–19).

To love our brothers does not necessarily mean to please them. Far from it. Nor does it mean that we must make a systematic effort to have them love us. On the contrary, it means that we must be capable, if necessary, of making them suffer for their own good. Therefore, we must sometimes be willing to fight them, individually and collectively.

It is on the basis of this concrete love, expressed in our actions, on the basis of this gift to others, even at the risk of misunderstandings and persecutions, that we will be judged. We must re-read in St Matthew how Christ himself describes the Last Judgement: '... I was hungry and you gave me food; I was thirsty and you gave me drink; I was a stranger and you made me welcome; naked and you clothed me, sick and you visited me, in prison and you came to see me ... I tell you solemnly, in so far as you did this to one of the least of these brothers of mine, you did it to me' (*Matt.* 25: 35–40).

What does it mean today, to feed the hungry? Does it mean to invite the old lady next door to supper, or to collect cans of condensed milk for the underdeveloped countries?

Yes, it means those things; but, more than that, it means to work in every agency to which we have access (trade unions, political parties and all the innumerable social groups to which we belong) for a decent living-wage for all, for fair prices, for job opportunities, for unemployment compensation, for pension plans, for job-training and so forth.

We know that the body can feel hunger, and we must come to recognise that the spirit can also be hungry. To feed the hungry spirit today means to work for equal education for all, equal opportunities, decent schools and effective curricula.

To make strangers welcome means, as it always has, to open one's home to others; but it means above all to fight for decent housing for the poor, and for housing allowances. It means to participate in tenant organisations, to organise recreation for young people in housing developments.

Visiting the sick means precisely that. But it also means fighting for increased benefits for the sick, and for the improvement of medical facilities, and it means supporting medical research to the extent that one is able.

Actually to visit the inmates of a prison is a work of mercy; but it is a greater work of mercy to work for a penal system which will reform and educate the prisoners, and for organisations which help freed convicts; to encourage programmes of education and re-education in the cities and throughout the country; to participate in crime-prevention and job-finding projects; to take an active interest in the formation of specialist educators and in the organisation of their unions.

It is also many other things. It is fighting against *anything which imprisons man*—that is, fighting on behalf of and alongside all those who are deprived of their freedom, from individuals who are the victims of their own fears to the underprivileged who are the collective prisoners of unjust economic, social and political structures.

15

Given the 'creeping socialism' of the modern world, human life has become more and more dependent upon those structures—so much so that it is now almost impossible to say that we truly love our brothers unless we are willing to participate in the creation of new structures, or in the transformation or reform of existing structures so as to obtain their greatest possible good.

'Charitable acts' can be misleading. They may allow us to believe that we are charitable. But, in fact, unless we are willing to take love seriously enough to make a reasonable and humanly effective commitment to the transformation of society, we risk falling under the judgement of God: 'Go away from me, with your curse upon you . . . For I was hungry and you never gave me food; I was thirsty and you never gave me anything to drink; I was a stranger and you never made me welcome, naked and you never clothed me, sick and in prison and you never visited me' (*Matt.* 25: 41–44).

There are men who teach, or allow others to believe, that a man can be saved if he merely observes the rules of sexual morality and the laws of the Church. Such men are either ignorant or dishonest.

Certainly, it is a good thing to help priests in their work by participating in parish activities and to be an active member of a Christian movement. It is good, but it is not enough, for it does not necessarily involve a commitment. Such activities, laudable as they are, *do not dispense a man from serving his brothers in the world*, for it is in the world that we have been placed by God's providence; and it is in the world that Christ awaits us.

To choose the form which our commitment will take means to take into account both our own talents and the needs of our brothers and of society, and then to go out to meet the Father halfway, in the midst of that society and those structures in which we spend our lives.

The choice of commitments must be a reasonable one.

We cannot do everything, but we must do whatever we can; and we must do it in a spirit of faith.

It is true that it also requires a commitment to the world in order for one to belong to a parent–teacher association, or to a union, or to a political party, or to an agency of student-government, or even to a social club. But it is also true that it requires a temporal commitment to feed the hungry and clothe the naked—and these are the things which Jesus solemnly stated were the express condition of our salvation.

The commitment of a Christian differs essentially from that of a non-Christian because of the faith which a Christian brings to bear on the end to be accomplished and, sometimes, by the means which he adopts. The end is Jesus, whom a man loves and serves by serving his brothers. He says, in effect: 'I love my neighbour as myself for love of Jesus.'

The means also take on a particular significance for the Christian, for he never forgets that, beyond and through the structures with which he deals, there are *persons* who must be liberated individually and collectively.

He does not manipulate these persons. Rather, he acts with them. He fights out of love, and not in the hope of a personal return for his efforts, or for purely material reasons, or out of rebelliousness, resentment or hate.

We should keep in mind, none the less, that a man who truly loves his brothers by working for them at the worldly level, *loves God without knowing it*, even though he has never encountered Jesus. In such a case, Christians should not try to claim a non-believer as one of their own. Instead, they should thank God for the love shown by the nonbeliever.

We Christians, because we know what is involved, are privileged creatures. We also bear a double responsibility. Why should we institutionalise our charity by participating in the work of those agencies and movements which are working for the common good? Because Jesus Christ asks us to love our brothers, and because loving our brothers today—without forgetting that they are *persons*—very often means creating and implementing structures at every level which will enable them to grow in justice and in love.

We are obliged to go to the very end in love of our brothers, but with the minds and hearts of men saved by Christ and living in him: 'I tell you solemnly, in so far as you did this to one of the least of these brothers of mine, you did it to me.'

5.

Lord, you are making my life very complicated!
Your commandment, 'You shall love the Lord your God'
    would have been much easier to obey,
if only you hadn't coupled it with another one, similar to it:
    'You must love your neighbours.'
        To love them all,
        All of the time—
That's not easy, Lord.
Even so, I thought I had done it.
I thought I was a good Christian and 'charitable to my neighbours'. Everyone thought I was
        so kind,
        so available,
        so devoted.
And now, you tell me that it was not enough.
And you even tell me that perhaps, sometimes, it was wrong!

It's hard, Lord, to love a neighbour that I can see;
But it's even harder to love one that I cannot see
        to work for brothers I do not know,
            and who do not know me;
        to fight alongside them, for them,
            against structures, and for structures
            which themselves are not my brothers
            but which make or unmake my brothers.

I would have preferred to have had a protégé of my very own, someone who needed my help,
On my very own road leading from Jerusalem to Jericho.
> Someone well cared for,
> And perhaps a bit spoiled,
> And in good health.
But the road from Jerusalem to Jericho has got longer and longer, and now it leads to the ends of the earth.
In fact, there are many such roads, all intersecting; they cover mankind, they stretch out into time, into what is and what is to be.
Lord, I am on my own small road now. I am moving forward, step by step.
One of my hands is for one brother; the other, for another.
I am too slow and too small to love all my brothers.

I am going to join the army of those who are fighting
And who, however painfully, in their organisations and their movements, their meetings and their encounters and their battles,
Are trying to build a world, Lord, in which man, free, will be able finally to love.

I am available, Lord,
> to you,
> for them.
I am available, brothers, even though I don't know who you are.

2. If Jesus read today's newspaper

Every morning, I glance at the newspaper. Then, in the evening, I read it thoroughly. I want to know what is happening. It is a duty. I know this, and I say so to everyone who will listen. Thus, on this point as on so many others, my conscience is at ease. I am up to date on world and national affairs, I tell myself. I care about what is happening. I have opinions, and I am able to hold my own in any discussion of affairs.

But suddenly, I have realised that there is not a great deal of difference between the way that I, a militant Christian, read the newspaper, and the way that any militant non-Christian reads it. If there is a difference, it must be deep within me, in my outlook. No one who really lives his faith can look upon the world from a purely human standpoint.

Because I am a Christian, I am 'of Christ', and I must imitate Christ. Even more, I must identify myself with him, become an extension of him. But if Jesus came down on earth today—after all, what are two thousand years of human history?—how would he read his newspaper? One thing I know, he would certainly read it. How could he possibly be indifferent to the news of the world? How could he possibly leave unopened the daily letters which reach everyone, and give them news of their brothers all over the world?

Jesus, first of all, would search out the most reliable sources;

those which, because they are less moved by passion, have the most respect for the truth which he loves.

But what would the news mean to Jesus—the news which millions of men, hungry for knowledge, study every day? What would he see in a daily chain of human events which are painful, joyful, discouraging, amusing, horrifying? Would he find in these things material for discussion, or for strong emotions, or for anger? He would find all of these in them. But, beyond human events, he would see the Kingdom of his Father being built or demolished. *Jesus, in reading his newspaper, would read the news of the Kingdom.* What is happening to my brothers, who are my living members? he would ask. Is my Body being built up? What were the problems yesterday, the failures and the successes? What will they be today?

And, with his newspaper in his hand, Jesus would pray to the Father.

Mankind does not have two histories, one spiritual and one worldly. There are not two lives for man, one human and the other Christian. There is only one history; only one life. In that history and that life, in the hearts of the sons of God, both the 'temporal' and the 'spiritual' are inextricably united although, in themselves, they are distinct. (I apologise for using such old-fashioned terms as temporal and spiritual; but, after all, one must use words, and these terms are the ones commonly employed.)

The man who lives by faith—that is, the man who is united to Jesus—has the gift of seeing the eternal dimension in everyday affairs.

I do not read my newspaper as a Christian should.

First of all, under the pretext that I must be 'up to date', I spend much too long over reading it. I linger over ridiculous but amusing items, while I merely glance at the important news and at the more formidable editorials and articles.

Then, when I have finished, I judge. And I judge severely.

Either I condemn others, or I congratulate myself on my political acumen. 'How could they have been so stupid?' I ask. Or I say: 'It happened exactly as I expected it would.'

I draw no meaningful lessons from my newspaper. I am content to remain at the surface of events. My strongest reaction is a faint shudder when I read about something particularly horrifying. Sometimes I say a distracted prayer in order to soothe my conscience and to maintain my self-respect.

Since the Lord wants me to be like him, he obviously demands more of me than that.

I am a friend of Jesus. 'I call you servants no longer, but friends.' I am a member of the family, a son, and I am involved in the establishment of the Kingdom. I am responsible for more than my own personal development. I am involved, with all my brothers, in the development of the entire human community. And my newspaper gives me daily news of that progress.

I must become capable of reading, not between the lines, but above the lines; for the total reality of events infinitely transcends their superficial meaning. I must develop a new way of looking at things, a 'double sight'; that of faith, which is the union of Jesus' outlook with my own, so that I may see beyond persons and beyond history.

If I am to learn to go beyond the visible shell of events, I must read the gospel regularly. If I do so faithfully, I will acquire the viewpoint of Jesus Christ—his cares, his reactions, his manner of seeing people, his outlook on the world.

If I persevere, I shall soon learn to find gospel values in human events—values which are the measure of progress in the building of the Kingdom: man's struggle for greater freedom, justice, responsibility and dignity for all individuals and all nations; everything which has to do with human progress, from unions for workers, the organisation of markets, construction and so forth, to education and art;

everything which works towards peace, unity, treaties, the peaceful settlement of conflicts . . .

By the same token, I shall also discover obstacles: certain political, economic and social events, unjust imprisonments, restraints on freedom of expression—or simply on freedom itself, striking examples of injustice, unemployment, lack of housing and of schools, the breaking off of relations between individuals and among nations, violence—and innumerable other things.

I must therefore do what Jesus would do. I must pray to the Father. I must ask for forgiveness of sins. I must thank him for such progress as is made in the establishment of the Kingdom. I must offer to him the whole of human effort made by men who may or may not know that they are participating, by every one of their acts, in the painful journey of the People of God towards the Promised Land.

If all Christians, every day, learn to overcome their curiosity and their emotions and to read their newspapers as children of God, they will learn to decipher the signals given them by Jesus. Then, their commitment will be not only the fruit of human reflection, but also an exciting journey towards beckoning love.

It is true that I cannot afford the time every day to make my reading of the newspaper the starting point of a serious meditation—I should, however, do so from time to time—but I can take a few minutes, or even a few seconds, every day, in the sight of my Father who watches me,

to offer, through Jesus Christ,
the whole of struggling mankind,
and the world which is moving slowly, so slowly,
towards eternal love.

Excuse me, Lord, for being so superficial.
I've wasted my time over earthly goods
and I haven't even started the long pilgrimage
which leads to you, living in the heart of human history.

23

But why are you hidden, Lord?
Why does your Holy Spirit,
    even when mysteriously at work among men,
    remain unknown to us?

I need to see you, Lord,
I need to hear you.
Strengthen my sight, and let me see the true meaning of
events,
So that I may know it is you when you give me a sign,
So that I may hear when you invite me to act.

'It is nearly evening, and the day is almost over.'
Stay with me, Lord,
    for night has fallen,
    and, too often, it is dark in my heart.
Stay with me,
    and in your Light I will read my newspaper as you
    would read it,
    and then get up and go out to my brothers.

3. God's children go to school

Our son Henry goes to the local primary school, and I belong to the Parent–Teacher Association. My husband is on one of the school committees. Our daughter Jeanne is at high school, and although she's not yet sure of what she wants to be, she says that she wants to go to college. I wonder if we'll be able to afford to send her? Right now, the odds are against it. And I must say that we don't have much incentive to make sacrifices for her education, because she isn't really a hard worker at school. Sometimes we punish her for being lazy; and we've used every argument we can think of to make her study harder.

My husband and I feel that we have to keep abreast of educational problems and to take an active part in our school organisations, so we try to read as much as we can on the subject. We've come to realise that there are a great many problems. And we realise too, that we have been continually trying to resolve these problems without examining them in the light of the Lord. Finally, yesterday we did so.

We know for certain that God takes an interest in the education of his children, just as he takes an interest in every aspect of their lives.

It is also certain that God wants everyone to attain a maximum degree of development not only in his son Jesus Christ, *but also at the natural level*. No father worthy of the name could conceivably be willing to accept the physical, intellectual or moral 'underdevelopment' of his children.

God, therefore, wants every man to be able normally to

attain at least a minimum of education; and that minimum must increase as civilisation progresses.

There is always a disparity of talents among the children of a family. They have different 'gifts'. The same holds true in the human family. God does not want everyone to be the same. He requires diversity. Every man is different, unique; and therein lies his greatness. None the less, every man must make full use of the talents which God has given him. Differences in education, therefore, should depend upon differences in ability, and not, as they often do, upon wealth and other irrelevant factors.

It is the duty of society, as a whole, to allow every man to develop in proportion to his gifts—that is, to fulfil God's individual plan for him. By the same token, the gifts of the Father to his children become the responsibility of those children. They must make those gifts bear fruit. This is an absolute condition, and we shall all have to render an account of the use we have made of them.

Thus, we are working in accordance with God's plan, and fulfilling his essential wish for the total development of every man and all men, when, according to our limited means, individually or collectively, we work, through the various associations and organisations to which we belong, for an increase in the world rate of literacy; for equal educational opportunities; for more, and more fairly distributed scholarships; for better schools and teachers; for a re-organisation of the educational system; and so for anything which encourages the maximum development of the individual.

What the Father wishes for his children is a balanced, integrated development. And, for that, it is necessary to have an educational system which produces real 'persons'. It is not a question of training dogs—i.e., of making children absorb the greatest possible amount of information—but of teaching human beings to think, to make sound judgements; and of giving each one of them what his individual needs require. This is what we are working for when we campaign for a more 'humanised' educational system, for participation by the students in their own education, for more rational curricula, for the abolition of cramming, etc.

The education and formation of young people is not an individual but a collective undertaking. It is God's work that students and teachers are joined in a single class, in a particular school or scholastic environment for several hours a day and for several years. These are natural groups, and God watches over them. He wants them to become communities open to his Love, and centres of personal development.

Since, in the mind of the Father, a class is a gathering in which the students and teacher are united, we should do everything possible to help the less gifted, to encourage work as a team, and to develop unity among the students themselves. For the same reason, we must oppose the formation of special groups or *cliques*, any unjustified disorder which would interfere with the work of the community, any dishonesty, any passivity, and anything which would promote the spirit of every-man-for-himself.

We have an obligation to make our classes and our schools succeed. The Christian, whether he is a student, teacher or parent, who tries to find the means to bring about that success and patiently makes use of those means, joins his actions to the action of God which is at work in the whole of human reality.

A young person, like all persons, is a 'whole'. He must be educated at the various levels of his being, including the spiritual level. When we allow our children to receive religious instruction, when we give them the opportunity to live their Christianity in their own environment, we are joining ourselves to God who, from all eternity, has wanted to make the children of men his own children.

All of society must become the Body of Christ, the Church of God. The schools are not isolated institutions within that society. They are not groups cut off from all other groups.

27

They depend on the whole of society, and they must be open to the whole of life.

Children belong first of all to those who made them: their parents. The parents have the responsibility for their education at every level of their being. They have no right to ignore that responsibility. If they leave the education of their children entirely in the hands of teachers and schools, they become parents who have at least partially 'abandoned' their offspring.

So far as God is concerned, there is no such thing as a single, solitary man. There are only individuals in various relationships with other individuals. In this instance, the individuals are the parents, the teachers and the students themselves, who are collectively responsible, in accordance with their individual roles, for the total development of young people.

Everyone belongs to a particular social environment by which he is profoundly influenced and moulded. At the same time, man is responsible for his environment. He has no right to ignore it, or to reject the natural (and, for a Christian, divine) ties which bind him to his environment. Students, teachers and academic institutions must all take that environment into account; for each environment has its own 'culture', which is a treasure, or a 'talent', which must not only not be ignored; it must also be developed. We cannot allow everyone to be treated exactly alike for we must allow everyone to develop in accordance with his background.

Every student has a real obligation to develop a 'professional conscience' about his studies. Most often, his education is being paid for by society—and especially by working-people. Students, in other words, are privileged beings, and as such they have responsibilities to society. They are responsible for preparing themselves conscientiously to take their proper places as workers, and also in the social and political arenas.

Finally, all those who participate in the educational system—and the students themselves, first of all—are responsible to mankind as a whole. They have an obligation with respect to the goals of improved education and the development of the minds of men. We must learn to look far into the distance; far beyond our own immediate and legitimate interests. Every man who enriches his mind contributes to mankind, allows mankind to take a step toward that 'spiritualisation' which is itself a step towards God. It is up to us Christians to place the whole of Christ's life squarely behind that movement forward.

We now understand better, Lord, why we should belong to parent–teacher associations.
We understand better why we must do everything we can for men to be able to obtain a true education: an education which is balanced, total, open and respectful of all the values of different environments and different communities.
We understand why, despite any obstacles, we must never cease educating ourselves.
And we have better reasons to give our children—really Christian reasons—why they should work hard in school.

> For they are your children, Lord.
> Your children go to school.
> Your children grow, and become adults.
> But how many of them will never develop fully?
>> How many of them will be permanently damaged?
> You don't want this to happen to any of them, Lord.
> We don't want it to happen either,
>> and that's why we want to fight
>> on your side, Lord.

4. I'm too good a neighbour

I was coming home from work the other evening when I ran into my neighbour in front of the house. 'I wonder if you'd have a minute to look at our washing-machine,' he asked. 'I don't seem to be able to get it started.'

'Of course,' I answered. 'Let me go in and tell my wife I'm home, then I'll come right over.'

A few minutes later, I was at work on his washing-machine. 'It must be nice to be handy,' he said. 'I can see that you know what you're doing.' I was delighted. It's a wonderful feeling to be admired and envied. As I gathered up my tools, I told him: 'That should do it. Let me know if you have any trouble. I'll be glad to come over any time.'

I went home in high good humour. I was happy because I had been 'charitable to my neighbour'. But a question from my wife destroyed my mood completely. 'Did you explain to him what was wrong with it,' she asked, 'so that, next time, he'll be able to fix it himself?'

I had not even thought of it. Perhaps because I was looking forward too much to the next opportunity I would have to show him how clever I was, and how 'charitable'.

The children were in bed. My wife, Georgette, and I were sitting at the table, talking about our attitude towards our neighbours.

We have the reputation among our friends (and in our own eyes) of being 'nice, helpful people'. Everyone knows that they can always count on us. It's the same way at my office, and, in fact, in my whole life.

I don't mean to say that that is bad. But we recognise that it is very limited, and very dangerous; and we have drawn the following conclusions:

We often derive enormous self-satisfaction from doing favours for people, and we are proud of what we regard as our 'neighbourliness'.

We often do things for our neighbours that we don't really want to do—and we do them only to preserve our self-esteem and not to lose our reputation as 'nice' people.

Above all, we tend to take the easy way out—i.e., to give *things* to our neighbours, while Jesus asks us to do something much more difficult: to help them to become self-sufficient, and (what is even harder) to give of themselves.

We had to think about it only a few minutes to discover many things in our lives that proved our attitude to be wrong. Georgette, for instance, spends a good deal of time running errands for an invalid woman in our building. She hasn't tried to get other neighbours to help, and she hasn't even thought of organising half-a-dozen of them in such a way that the invalid would have a different helper every day.

I'm no better. Sometimes, I do my son's homework for him instead of helping him to do it himself.

Georgette sometimes bakes a cake for a friend of hers on the third floor. But she's never thought of giving her the 'secret' recipe so that she can make it for herself. And she knits scarves and sweaters for us—but she hasn't bothered to teach our daughter how to knit.

Neither of us has ever asked our neighbours to help *us* with any of our problems.

Just a few days ago at work, I spoke to my employer on behalf of one of my fellow workers. It never occurred to me that I should have encouraged him to speak for himself, or at least to come with me while I spoke for him. And there have been innumerable instances of this kind.[1]

1. This chapter is not concerned with collective action in unions, political organisations, etc., not because such action is irrelevant, but because the

Jesus acted very differently when he walked among men.

At Cana, he turned water into wine—but not until the water had been drawn by the servants of the house.

When he spoke to the Samaritan woman, he began by asking her for a service: a drink of water.

When he wished to feed the people, he started with the bread and the fishes that a boy in the crowd had given him.

And of Zacchaeus, he demanded a place to stay.

Jesus, in other words, used the same methods as his Father. The Father insists on involving us in his work. With him, we must complete the creation of the universe by our work, and the creation of mankind by means of the family. If the Father acted alone, the work, no doubt, would be more perfect—but man would be less great.

The mystery of the Creation and that of the mystically continuing Incarnation and Redemption of Christ require our free participation if they are to be realised in human history. It is God and man, together, who are building the Kingdom.

We, however, have not used the methods of the Father.

How humiliating it is to need other people, and how satisfying it is to be needed by others. Too often, we keep our friends in a state of dependence on us. Even if they are willing to accept that arrangement, either out of laziness or because they do not recognise the situation for what it is, we do not have the right to impose it without offering them, at the same time, the opportunity to grow.

Christians must not be those who 'have' and who 'take care'of the have-nots. We must be men who come as equals, to share what we have.

We must not be men who are always needed, but men who sometimes need others.

---

family in question is not politically oriented. What we were doing in this particular meeting was trying to make this couple overcome their paternalistic attitude towards their neighbours.

We must not be men who are always giving, but men who also lead others to give.

When we give someone something, he has something which he did not have before. But so far as he himself is concerned, he has not been changed.

When, on the other hand, we help someone to become a better person, we allow him to become more a man—a free and generous son of God, as the Father intends him to be. And what greater service can we render a man than to make him more of a man?

Every time that we teach someone how to give, even if it is through the smallest gesture in our everyday lives, we lead him on to the path of the Father; we join ourselves to the great redeeming effort of Jesus by releasing man from the slavery of sin and making of him Jesus' friend, his collaborator in the building of the Kingdom, in Love.

Lord, we've fallen into the habit of always being neighbourly. We're the St Bernards of everyone we run into. We know what to say,
> when to smile,
> what to do.

Yes, Lord, we're good and faithful servants; but we'll never learn to be more than that

As long as, without knowing it, and because of us,
> other people remain unimportant while we remain important,
> they remain poor while we hold on to our wealth;
> and we don't know what to do with ourselves if ever they don't need us any more.

Help us, Lord, to be good neighbours, but without loving
> less than we should.

Help us to make others grow large and ourselves grow smaller,
> by giving less and asking more,

by making saviours out of other people instead of
being saviours ourselves.
If we can do that, Lord, then
    we won't be benefactors,
    and we won't be father-figures,
        we'll be brothers to our brothers.

5. I want to be Somebody

The other day, my sister, in the heat of an argument, said to me: 'The trouble with you is that you have no personality!'

That upset me a great deal. Nothing hurts me more than to be told that I'm dull and uninteresting, because my greatest ambition has always been to be *somebody*—a 'personality', exciting and stimulating to be with.

I've thought over the problem, especially with reference to my sister. She's younger than I, and she hasn't had the education I've had. She's less intelligent than I, and she hasn't the variety of talents that I have. And yet, she is a leader. She knows how to get things done, and how to get others to do what she wants. Some of her friends come to her with their problems, and she is somehow able to find the right things to say, so that they go away feeling better. I'm very different.

Torn between jealousy of my sister—whom, none the less, I love very much—and my restless search for a way to become *somebody*, a leader, a personality, it seems that I've never bothered to acquire the insight that only faith can give. It never occurred to me that God could be interested in my struggle to be important.

This evening, I talked the whole thing over with my parish priest. Now, I see it more clearly, and I feel much better. Now that I am no longer so worried, perhaps I can find the means to become what I want to be. My ambition is perfectly legitimate, but I have been wrong in the way I went about fulfilling it. I will have to find other means.

And, above all, I will have to go about it in an entirely different spirit.

My first mistake has been to confuse personality and originality. As a youngster, very often merely to have my own way, to make my own ideas prevail, I treated the ideas of others with contempt. I thought that in attracting attention to myself, in making myself stand out, I was showing originality—and, therefore, personality.

By the same token, I began to copy people whose minds or behaviour I admired. It was as though I was trying to borrow a personality instead of developing one of my own.

Also, during an extended period of rebellion, I wanted to 'be myself'—but in my own way; that is, to follow even my most ridiculous ideas, to express my immediate reactions, to follow my impulses and what I regarded as my 'instincts'. I thought I was free. But a mature personality is harmonious and well integrated, and controls its emotions in order to channel them—and I was merely disorganised and scatter-brained.

At present, I have fallen into the practice of maintaining a careful silence which, to others, must seem somewhat mysterious. The fact is, I don't speak for fear of being misunderstood and laughed at. It is as though I am paralysed. I am afraid to speak or to act—and my silence and inactivity allows me to pass myself off as a wise and subtle man. But now I know that my limitations are of my own making.

I know that, beyond myself, there is someone—a person who is held prisoner within me and who is being slowly asphyxiated.

I know that the reason for my failure has been that, out of pride, I wanted, solely through my own efforts, to become someone; to become a god, but without God.

Today, my outlook was purified. I have re-discovered the One whose only wish, from all eternity, is to make me one of his children.

36

My personality is that which, within myself, makes me unique among men.

>It is God's concept of me.
>It is God's image in me.
>It is God's love for me—an individual and 'personal' love.

Since my birth, I have had, like every other man, a personality which is different, irreplaceable and which cannot be duplicated. It was given to me in its pristine form, like a piece of marble handed to an artist who must gradually impose on it the shape he has conceived. But I have not given it that shape. Instead, I have worked at it clumsily, disfiguring and deforming it.

I cannot fully develop my personality unless I am linked to all men, who are my brothers; for I am a member of a Body. I belong to a certain time in history, to a certain country, to a particular family and social class and I must develop in accordance with that environment.

I can develop my personality fully only if I collaborate with Jesus. If I work at it merely at the human level, I will remain incomplete, if not permanently deformed. *I must become the man whom the Father has planned from all eternity.*

I am infinitely more wealthy than I ever thought possible, for I am beyond price. I am unique, and therefore irreplaceable.

Other people need me. But they need the real me, and not the 'personality' that I've tried to manufacture; for what there is in me that is unique is precisely what they must have. If I continue playing games with myself, I am robbing them of what they need. If I offer them something artificial, I am leaving them as hungry as I found them. If I am not *myself*, something—someone—will be lacking in mankind and in the Body of Christ.

To develop my personality means to establish harmony among my gifts and talents by placing them at the service of Jesus in my brothers. The more I am what Jesus wants me to be, the more that I conform to his plan for me in my daily life, then the more I will have a personality of my own.

Finally, I will become a real 'personality'—when I am filled with Jesus, that is. For, far from undervaluing human nature and trying to discount my talents, Jesus offers me the opportunity to make them truly god-like by allowing their supreme development.

From this standpoint, which is that of faith, I am in a position to understand the true purpose, and the true grandeur, of education. It is to work with a child so as to discover in him the imprint of the living God and, gradually, in close collaboration with Jesus, to develop the authentic character of the son of whom the Father has dreamed from the beginning of time.

Now that I understand this, I must change my attitude towards other people. What right have I to impose my own ideas on them and to set up my own behaviour as a model for them? My duty is not to lead them, or to train them, but, first of all, to respect them. I must respect what they are in themselves, the individual mystery of each one of them, and God's plan for them in which I must cooperate in all humility.

Every person has something to give me. What is unique in them is necessary to me. In the presence of another, I am always poor; for the other person always possesses a treasure which I lack.

Lord, tonight I ask you, once and for all, to rid me of my concern about the impression I make on other people.

Forgive me
> for being so preoccupied
> with what I seem to be,
> with the effect I produce,
> with what others think and say of me.

Forgive me
>for wanting to imitate others to the extent that I forget who I am,
>
>for envying their talents so much that I neglect to develop my own.

Forgive me
>for the time I spend playing games with my 'personality' and for the time I don't spend in developing my character.

Now, let me forget about the stranger that I was
>so that I may find myself;
>
>for I will never know my home unless I leave it,
>and I will never find myself if I refuse to lose myself.

Lord, let me be open to my brothers,
>so that, through them, you will be able to visit me as your friend.

For then I will be the person that your Love wants me to be,
>your son, Father,
>and a brother to my brothers.

6. On God's track

I'm discouraged again.

I've done my best to be of help to my brothers in my personal contacts: at work, among my neighbours at home, everywhere and with everyone, by total commitment. I was told that I had to do this in order to be a real Christian. I believed it. I still believe it. I had hoped that my activities would be the beginning of an apostolic career. It seems, however, that I've had no success at all. Just this afternoon, I was overwhelmed by the suspicion that I was working for nothing, that I was wasting my time, that Jesus didn't depend on my work to reveal himself, and that the Kingdom of the Father could be built perfectly well without me.

Thinking about it later, I discovered what had happened to crystallise my sense of discouragement. It began with a stupid sermon last Sunday at mass. The priest's words have been in my mind since then, making me uneasy and giving strength to the periodic temptation to give it all up.

I don't even know who the priest was, since he was only 'helping out' for that weekend. I recall vividly, however, that for a solid fifteen minutes he kept repeating that the world was rotten and that we had to withdraw from it as quickly as possible so that we could pray and make sacrifices in solitude. 'Above all,' he said, 'avoid the tragic mistake made by those who plunge into the active life, and thereby ruin their interior lives and sow only the wind . . .'

I am as shocked by that sermon today as I was on Sunday. The people in church did not need to be urged not to give themselves to others. Rather, they needed to be told the reasons why they *should* give themselves. None the less, instead of spending the rest of the mass formulating a few cutting remarks I might have made to the priest after the service, it would have been better for me first of all to go and discuss the matter with him. (As it happened, I ended up doing absolutely nothing about it, on the pretext that it wouldn't have done a bit of good.) Secondly, I should have searched out something that, in spite of everything, applied to myself in that horrible sermon. For it's undeniable that, before committing myself to the active life, I was more *conscious* of Jesus in my life. Now, busy as I am, and constantly occupied with one thing and another, I sometimes lose sight of him. I want to reveal him to men, but he is silent and remains hidden. There are times when I feel an urge to leave my brothers and try to find him again. Is this a temptation? I've discussed it with a friend of mine who is a priest.

At the present time, I am trying to work as hard as I can for the salvation of my brothers. And, when I speak of salvation, I mean total salvation. I feel certain that I should continue on this path. I would be a hypocrite if, every night, I asked the Father to let men and society become more just and loving, and yet refused to work during the day to make them so.

The fact that I am so often discouraged is because my work is not sufficiently founded on faith. I struggle too much at the purely human level. I work too much alone, without offering my work to Jesus, and, even worse, without keeping in mind that *Jesus is inviting me, in the midst of my life, to work at his side*.

Jesus did not wait for me to begin his work in the world. He died, it is true; but then he rose from the dead. Moreover, his Holy Spirit came down at Pentecost, as Jesus had promised; and no one has ever said since then that the Spirit left the earth and returned to the Father.

The risen Jesus permeates human life, but he remains hidden. How can I know that he is really there? How can I be sure that it is not all an illusion? First of all, because Jesus is where he promised he would be. For he has spoken; and to 'have faith' is to believe Jesus, to accept him at his word.

I should read the gospels and listen to Jesus. He said it without reservation: 'I am with you always; yes, to the end of time.'

He said: 'When a few of you are gathered together in my name, I will be there among you.' And whenever I am together with my brothers in Jesus, not only to pray but also to discuss my work in the service of mankind, I know that Jesus is there also, *because he has told me so.*

After having commanded us to love one another, Jesus said: 'If anyone loves me he will keep my word, and my Father will love him, and we shall come to him and make our home with him.' When my friends and I try to practise brotherly love in our lives, Jesus and the Father are in us. *Jesus has said so.*

Jesus, speaking of the Last Judgement, told us that he had been hungry, thirsty, homeless, naked, ill, in prison. He identified himself with the poor, with those who are poor in worldly goods, in health, in freedom—in other words, with all those who are deprived. Whenever I meet someone who is poor, poor in any sense of the word, it is Jesus whom I meet. Jesus himself has told me so.

When we see a rose blooming in the middle of a thicket, we say: A rosebush is growing there. When I see the words of the gospel blooming in human life, faith tells me: 'Jesus is there, mysteriously at work in the hearts of men.' By the same token, when I see a bit of love, of unity, of justice or of freedom in other people, in a certain environment, in events or structures, I know that Jesus is there, present by his action among men.

Finally, when I find sin within myself or in others, or in

the whole of life, my faith tells me that it is Jesus who is at work there too. He is there because he has taken all sins upon himself and borne them for us. He has bought us back. But this redemption, although fully realised two thousand years ago, is unfolding today in human history.

St Paul tells us that we are saved 'in hope'. But we are saved every day 'in act' when we encounter our Liberator; when we open ourselves to him and work with him.

To be a Christian means to encounter Jesus, to know him, to believe what he has said, to love him. But it also means to recognise him in one's own life and to participate with him in the mystery of creation and of his redemptive incarnation.

After a rational analysis of the situation, I joined in the struggle in order to serve my brothers. But my outlook of faith, above and beyond my human outlook, is what allows me to see Jesus mysteriously at work. Jesus signals to me through human events. Thus, my own action is joined humbly to his.

Of course, I can misinterpret Jesus' signals, but there are two ways in which I can learn to read them more accurately. One is to discover, in the gospels, what were Jesus' ways of doing things and of behaving. The other is to search for these ways with others, as a team, in the Church.

The active life, therefore, is not an obstacle to an encounter with Jesus. Rather, it is a meeting place with him. But, in the midst of my activities, I must constantly accept Jesus' invitation to talk to him. This is the real 'living prayer'.

How can I preach Jesus to my brothers? Often, I must accept having to work alongside him while he remains hidden and unknown. But if I know him and recognise him in life, if I consciously work with him, it may be that others will come to realise that I am not working alone. Certainly, I could speak his name. I don't want to do so too often, and I should not forget that my role is limited to *speaking* of him. Only Jesus himself can *reveal* himself.

I must prepare the way for the Lord, and become the light
on the road by which he will come.

Lord, forgive the ignorance and the fear of those who
try to hide in sacristies, convents and churches.
　　But forgive me, too,
　　because I know that you are with us and among us, and
　　I often forget it.

Lord, why must we always be looking at the surface of
things and events which we do not understand?
　　And why can't I receive your Light
　　in such a way that it illuminates the whole world and
　　every step of my way?
Why can't I be the 'seer' who discovers you, hidden, needy,
among us?
Why can't I be one of those who gather the blossoms of the
gospel in the evening and present them to you?

Lord, make me understand
　　that I must not run away from the world,
　　　　since you are waiting for me in the world;
　　that there is no need for me to put you in contact with
　　life,
　　　　since you are already present among men, who
　　　　are my brothers;
　　that, far from fleeing the active life,
　　　　I should just join in your Action among men.

Grant, Lord, not that I may see the obstacles to your coming
into the world, but above all that I may know
　　　　where to meet you,
　　　　how to recognise your signals,
　　　　and your invitations,
and if, some day, I speak your name, let it not be to speak of
a distant, inaccessible, unknown and unknowable God,

but to introduce you as my friend, Lord,
    as my companion-in-arms,
    and of course as a transcendent God,
    but as God present and acting in the world.

For you have risen, Lord, and your Holy Spirit is at work
in human history
    to increase your whole Body,
    to build the Kingdom of the Father,
    to construct your Church.

'There is one among you whom you do not know.'
        I'm sorry, Lord, I didn't know it was you.
'The Kingdom of God is among you.'
        Forgive me, Lord. I had forgotten.
'I am with you always; yea, to the end of time.'
        Again, Lord, I'm sorry. I've behaved as though
        I were alone in our Father's vineyard.

7. A Father's gifts

It was still early. I was on my way home from a meeting and, for the first time, I wasn't in a hurry. I made a detour to walk along the sea shore, and I stopped to look at the water. It was a calm, beautiful night.

Leaning against the railing, I could hear the cars behind me in the street, their horns blaring impatiently. The drivers seemed all in a hurry to get somewhere. I experienced a moment of irritation. How blind they were to the beauty that lay just beside the road, I told myself. But, before I could pass judgement on their blindness, I brought myself up short. For it occurred to me that I was really no better than they. How smug I felt because I had taken a few minutes to admire the sea! Yet, how often did I pause long enough to do so?

The full moon shone through a gathering of dark clouds and made a shimmering path across the water to the shore. In its light, the waves gathered, rolled, and finally broke on the sand.

I watched, and a feeling of peace took possession of my mind. I relaxed, and I was filled with silent admiration.

'Thank you, Lord,' I prayed, 'for all the beauty that you have given us.'

Then, I realised that it was not enough for me to admire God's work and to thank him for it. I must also help nature by lending it my heart and my lips so that, through me, it might praise the Creator. Looking at the ocean which, every night and every day, radiates beauty without knowing it, without being able to offer that beauty to God, I was filled with fear that there were not enough contemplatives in the world to thank God for the universe that he has given us.

The joy of a father consists entirely in the excitement of a child over a gift. The delight in the child's face is a reflection of the gratitude which permeates his mind and body. It is the child's prayer of thanksgiving.

Into the hands of mankind God has placed a marvellous gift: the universe. Man, since his hands are still clumsy, has not yet been able to open all of God's presents. But he grows with each passing day; and, each day, he discovers new gifts, learns to use them, to master them and to transform them.

When, finally, the Father saw his children playing with the atom, painstakingly trying to make use of it, to harness the incredible power which had been hidden there since the beginning of time, he was filled with joy. But how many of his children thanked him for this gift? They were too busy making weapons out of it, to kill their brothers.

The greatest insult we can offer to God is to use what he gives us to perpetrate injustice (to monopolise God's gift, without regard for our brothers) or to engage in fratricidal wars (all wars, general or 'limited').

Personally, I control—or at least I should control—this piece of matter which I call my body. It is intelligent. It is filled with the love of Jesus, with a sense of the divine. It is transfigured. And thus, it will participate in the love of the Trinity.

The body which I occupy needs other matter: the air, the sun and the things around me which I use. I free these things of their opacity by lending them my soul, as it were. They need me. The universe has need of me in order to free itself of its purely material nature.

The sea, the moon and the chilling wind, all need to be offered to God. Left to themselves, they are incapable of raising themselves to the level of the spirit. They are beautiful, but they do not know it. They beautify the world, refresh it, inspire in it a sense of peace; but they cannot *will* to do so. They do not have the power, of themselves, to rise to their Creator, to praise him by offering him loving thanks for their beauty. To do so requires the human mind, human consciousness, human freedom, and a human heart.

I am allowed to look at, to desire, and to make use only of what I am capable of giving. I cannot look, and then take something only for myself; for then I would be interrupting its majestic ascent towards God for whom it was made.

It is *not* an act of Christian virtue to refuse to take something. It *is* an act of Christian virtue to refuse to keep something. To be a Christian does not mean to seize and to plunder. It means to give.

I will have to train my senses, which are the 'hands' of my soul, not to make prisoners of things: and it is a course of training which will never really end.

I must learn to appreciate and to thank God not only for the sea, the stars, the trees and the flowers, but also for the world which man, with God, has transformed: for the houses and streets; for the ultra-modern factory, shining with ten thousand lights, which stretches along the highway; for rockets and man-made satellites—for the whole of that technology by means of which man, whether he knows it or not, joins with his Creator in the act of creation.[1]

Matter is good, since it is the work of God and the fruit of his creative love.

The Word was made *flesh*; and flesh—matter and life— became part of eternity through the Word and with the Word.

The whole of the universe, following in the footsteps of Christ the Saviour, is to participate in the resurrection: 'The whole creation is eagerly waiting for God to reveal

1. Often, we must also ask God's forgiveness, unfortunately, for building the world in such a way that it crushes man by alienating him. We are certainly aware of that aspect of human technology; but the purpose of this piece is to meditate on an obligation which we almost always choose to ignore: that of praising God.

his sons. It was not for any fault on the part of creation that it was made unable to attain its purpose, it was made so by God; but creation still retains the hope of being freed, like us, from its slavery to decadence, to enjoy the same freedom and glory as the children of God. From the beginning till now the entire creation, as we know, has been groaning in one great act of giving birth' (*Rom.* 8: 19–22).

Will there be, in the modern world, a sufficient number of men who are free from all injustice, who are sufficiently capable of astonishment, to stop, look at and admire nature, and science, and technology? Will there be men like Francis of Assisi who, by the way in which they live their lives, will add a new verse to the Hymn of Creation?

We praise you, Father, for the sea, the sky and the stars.
We praise you for the power of the atom.
We praise you for the oil flowing like rivers,
　　for the rockets like lightning among the stars,
　　for the satellites hovering over the planets.
We praise you, Father for science and technology.
We praise you for the matter which you have created,
　　which, though it seems dead to our eyes,
　　is yet living matter,
　　matter transformed,
　　the meeting-place of divine action and human activity.

We praise you, Father, for the artists and technicians,
　　for the scholars and the countless workers
　　who take that matter, and use it, and transform it.
We praise you for the Eternal Plan of your love,
　　which governs that great movement forward of the universe.

We praise you for your Son. Through him all things came to be, and not one thing has its being but through him. Through him, you continue to create all things,

to make them holy,
to give them life,
to bless them,
and to give them to us.
It is by him, and with him, and in him,
God the Father almighty,
and in the unity of the Holy Spirit,
that we honour you and glorify you.
for ever and ever.

Lord, let me be the one who, from time to time,
in the still of the night,
looks with the eyes of a son
upon what you have created,
so that I may praise the Creator.
Let me be as an excited child before the Father,
so that he may smile down upon the child that I am.

8. Finding my place in the work of creation

Yesterday, I went to a career-guidance centre. I didn't want to go, but my parents insisted and kept after me until I went.

I had talked it over with my friends. One of them had gone to the centre and taken the aptitude tests. He hadn't been very happy with the results. He was advised not to enter certain trades, and then, in very general terms, to think of going to work in such and such an area.

Without really knowing what it was all about, and without having thought much about it, I had already made up my mind that career-guidance was a waste of time.

I spent the morning taking tests and making critical comments to myself about them, ridiculing the idea that, from the way that I underlined words and analysed geometric patterns, they would be able to tell what kind of work I was cut out for. And, when I was interviewed, I thought the interviewer's questions both too personal and silly. By then, I was in a bad mood, and I answered them curtly.

Last night I went over the whole thing with my discussion group, and I applied to myself, personally, the essentials of what we discovered together.

First of all, I've come to realise that I was reacting impulsively, without thinking, and that I allowed myself to be confirmed in my impulsiveness by the equally irrational opinions of my friends. I echoed their reactions without making any effort to arrive at a sound judgement. I merely dismissed the whole idea of career-guidance without having any good reasons for doing so.

This was not the behaviour of an intelligent man, let alone that of a son of God. Lord, it was not what you expected of me.

Once more, the fact that I had not made a reasonable judgement led me to behave badly towards others. I was received courteously at the guidance centre. The people there were kind and thoughtful, and my interviewer was obviously doing his best for me. But my own behaviour was barely polite.

In other words, Lord, I behaved badly towards you. For it was you who were attempting to guide me, to enlighten me by means of the intelligence, knowledge, experience and words of those who were trying, in spite of me, to help me.

Finally and above all, I realise now that, so far as a career is concerned, I have been led only by self-interest. It never occurred to me that my choice was important to God and to my brother-men. 'What do you want to do?' How often I've been asked that question. And, most often, my reaction was one of irritation—because, to tell the truth, I didn't know *what* I wanted to do.

My choice, till now, has been based on purely selfish considerations: What would *I* like to do? How can I earn the most money? And the only obstacles I foresaw were the possibility that I might not have the talent for a particular profession, or that my parents would not be able to afford to pay for my studies.

You see, Lord, that you had no place in my choice; and the question of whether or not I would be able to serve my brothers in any given profession never even entered my mind.

I've approached one of the most important aspects of my life—the choice and preparation of a career—as though your love had not been gently leading me from all eternity. And yet, I should have known that a loving father could not be indifferent to the material future of his child. So, how could you, eternal Father, not care what I did with my life in the world?—you who have 'blessed us with all the spiritual blessings of heaven in Christ' and who, before the world was made, 'chose us, chose us in Christ, to be holy and spotless, and to live through love' (*Eph.* 1: 4).

If I hadn't finally stopped and thought about it today, I would have chosen alone. I would have decided, without you, what to do with my life. I might have come to you after having made my choice and asked you to ratify it; but that would have been all. I might even have asked you to help me realise my plan: 'Our Father, who art in heaven . . . *my* will be done.'

What I was about to do was to reverse our roles. I was acting as though I were God. What I regarded as a praiseworthy effort to enlist your help was nothing more than an absurd and selfish attempt to use your power in order to carry out my own decisions and plans.

I am, of course, free and responsible. You've made me so, Lord. But freedom does not lie in the ability to do whatever I want in any way that I want. Freedom, for someone who loves, is a willing compliance with the legitimate desires of the one who is loved.

You have a certain plan for me, a loving and eternal idea. You want me to take part in the building of your Kingdom. It's up to me freely to consent to your plan. Then, I will be able to work as hard as I can for mankind. I will be able to use the gifts you have given me, and I will attain the level of development that you intend for me.

Yesterday, Lord, through the intermediary of the career-guidance centre, you asked me to discover the plan devised by your infinite love for me. And what did I do? I ran away.

Seen in the light of faith, career guidance consists in the use of certain human techniques to find the place and the work that you want for every man in the competition of your creation by human work. The tests are the means of discovering in detail the gifts that you have given us, the gifts which we must make bear fruit until you ask for an accounting. '. . . A man on his way abroad summoned his servants and entrusted his property to them. To one he gave five talents, to another two, to a third one, each in proportion to his ability . . .' (*Matt.* 25: 14–30). The search for a career, or for a new job, is part of the struggle to find a meaningful place in the world according to the just needs of the human community, and also an expression of the will to develop creation harmoniously and to see every man, free and responsible, in his proper place.

In this perspective, everyone can help to carry out your plan for the world:

the sociologists at their desks, when they determine accurately the economic and social needs of mankind;

the psychologists, career-guidance officers and counsellors, when they help men to discover the work they are capable of doing;

the trade unions, politicians, statesmen—all those who help mankind move forward by making it possible for all young people to choose their professions, prepare for them, and work in them.

Father, let them all become aware that they are your willing collaborators in the work of creation.

Lord, today I ask your forgiveness
> for the places that will remain empty in your vineyard,
> for needs that are created artificially,
> for talents that will never be developed
>> through the fault of man and the society he has created,
> for the countless workers, your sons, who will be deprived of the development that you want them to have,
> for my own lack of fervour in trying to find out what you want of me,

and for my lack of generosity in neglecting to try as hard as I can to be what you want me to be.

Lord, I thank you
for the talents you've given me,
for the physical and intellectual gifts I've received,
for the education I've received,
for the opportunities I have to choose the profession that I want.

Lord, let me be like putty in your hands.
Let me accept your guidance through events, so that conscious of the real needs of my brothers,
I may discover:
where you are waiting for me,
and the part that you want me to play,
through my work,
in the completion of your creation.

9. My neighbour and I

I'm not very pleased with myself. I've already gone over my attitude towards others several times, and now I realise that from the human standpoint my reactions are childish, while from the Christian standpoint, they are abnormal. And yet, I know that my behaviour towards my brothers will be what I am judged on. Before his death, Jesus told us: 'I give you a new commandment: love one another; just as I have loved you' (*John* 13: 34).

My dissatisfaction began this morning while I was reading the newspaper. The first headline I saw concerned a particularly terrible crime, and my reaction was one of total condemnation of the *persons* involved—condemnation mixed with a feeling of hatred.

I am horrified by such crimes. That is normal enough. But what right do I have to condemn the criminals? Is it my place, and do I have the ability, to determine their degree of responsibility? Even more, to my so-called desire for justice I've added another sin: hatred.

I've confused evil with those who do evil, and I've included both in a facile and self-righteous judgement.

I had better make a careful examination of conscience.

Looking back, I can see that my judgement of other people is often influenced by numerous outside factors. Only rarely am I able to be fully objective.

My emotions often cloud my vision. My judgement of another's opinions, attitudes, acts and accomplishments is favourable or unfavourable according to whether I like or dislike that person. In any discussion, if I am hurt by something that someone says, I regard that person as my adversary and I am automatically opposed to anything he says.

My views on politics, labour and society in general, as well as those of my friends and of my environment, play an important part in my judgements. There are certain well-defined categories in my mind, and even before I get to know anyone, or as soon as he opens his mouth, I place him in one of those categories. He is 'middle-class', or 'working-class'. He is a 'conservative', or a 'liberal'. He is 'committed' or 'uncommitted'; 'with it' or hopelessly 'square'. What he says, does, thinks are all interpreted according to the category in which I have placed him. What is worse, my attention and my efforts to exchange ideas with him are proportionate to his rank in *my* hierarchy of values.

It is hard to consider a man in himself, objectively, and not as an ally or an adversary, a neutral or an enemy. It is very hard to overcome my ideas, my prejudices, my emotion. And it is hardest of all, while starting at the human level, to rise above it and to see others as Jesus saw them.

Jesus was not without emotions; quite the contrary. But his judgements and his actions were not dictated by them. He preferred John to the other apostles, and he was not afraid to show it. 'The disciple Jesus loved was reclining next to Jesus' (*John* 13: 23). But when it came to choosing the first head of the Church, he selected, not the apostle he loved most, but the one he judged to be most suitable: 'So I now say to you: You are Peter, and on this rock I will build my Church' (*Matt.* 16: 18).

The men whom Jesus met were of different social classes and of widely varying opinions—but this did not affect the way he treated them. His only consideration was the Kingdom of his Father.

He healed the poor and the helpless: 'As Jesus went on his way, two blind men followed him shouting, "Take pity on us, Son of David." . . . Then he touched their eyes . . . And their sight returned' (*Matt.* 9: 27–30).

But he also helped the powerful: '. . . Up came one of the officials, who bowed low in front of him and said, "My daughter has just died, but come and lay your hand on her and her life will be saved." Jesus rose and, with his disciples, followed him' (*Matt.* 9: 18–19).

Jesus is available to everyone, regardless of their opinions, their race, or their place in society.

He condemned the Pharisees as 'whitened sepulchres'—but when one of them invited him to his house, Jesus accepted. 'One of the Pharisees invited him to a meal. When he arrived at the Pharisee's house and took his place at table . . .' (*Luke* 7: 36).

He also ate and drank with publicans and sinners (*Luke* 5: 30).

He spoke to the Samaritan woman, who belonged to a race despised by the Jews (*John* 4: 1–43).

He healed the servant of an officer in the army of occupation. 'When he went into Capernaum a centurion came up and pleaded with him. "Sir," he said, "my servant is lying at home paralysed, and in great pain." "I will come myself and cure him," said Jesus' (*Matt.* 8: 5–7).

Jesus treated sinners with disconcerting kindness. He hated sin, since sin would cost him his life; but he loved and welcomed sinners. In the presence of the woman caught in adultery, Jesus was silent and, out of courtesy, he lowered his eyes so as not to embarrass her. It was only when he was alone with her that he spoke and told her that she was forgiven. 'Jesus bent down and started writing on the ground with his finger. As they persisted with the question, he looked up and said, "If there is one of you who has not sinned, let him be the first to throw a stone at her." . . . When they heard this, they went away one by one, beginning with the eldest . . . "Neither do I condemn you," said Jesus, "go away and don't sin any more"' (*John*, 8: 6–11).

On the cross, he did not condemn the thieves crucified with him, even though they were almost certainly guilty. He listened in silence to the insults of one of them; and to the one who prayed, he said, 'I promise you, today you will be with me in paradise' (*Luke* 23 : 43).

What did he think of those who were putting him to death? What punishment did he plan for them? 'Father, forgive them; they do not know what they are doing.'

And of sinners in general, he said, 'I did not come to call the virtuous, but sinners' (*Matt.* 9: 12).

If I want to be able to behave towards others as Jesus behaved, I will have to learn to see them through the eyes of faith.

At present, I see those around me only through the eyes of my body. I see their colouring, their features. I hear their voices. I touch their skin. This is the 'sight' of my senses. I limit myself to this kind of contact, and my judgement of people is always superficial, and often wrong.

The Lord has given me another way of seeing, the faculty of intelligence. My mind enables me to go beneath the surface. I am able to recognise faces, to call someone by name, to recall the past. And by means of speech my mind can make contact with the minds of other men. This 'second sight', however, is not perfect. My contact with other men is subject to misinterpretation and error.

There is yet another way, a 'third sight': that of faith. It is very different from the other two, but no less real. It enables me to perceive the dimension of infinity within a person. That is, through faith I 'see' another as God himself sees him.

No matter who is before me, I know that he is a creature of the Father and that he was created by the Father in his own image; that is, that he is spirit as well as flesh, that he too is a creator and capable of freedom and love. Even though he may have been damaged by life and sin, there necessarily remains in him that reflection of divinity which is God's mark on him, the Almighty's eternal appeal to him to rise above himself, the infinite love of the Father beckoning to him.

In my sight, the other man, whether he knows it or not, is always a man who has been saved by Jesus. He is perpetually invited to become in fact what he is by right: the son of God.

As a son of God, he is also the brother of Jesus, a member of his entire Body, and a brother to all other men.

It is in this way that God sees and loves every man: as a member of his Son. And if a particular member is no longer alive, but has been killed by sin, then his love works even harder—if that is possible—to save him.

There is a man before me, Lord.
I am trying to see him as he really is,
    beyond my likes and dislikes,
    beyond my opinions and his opinions,
    beyond my behaviour and his behaviour.

I am trying to let him exist before my eyes
    as he exists within himself,
    and not force him to attack,
        or to defend,
        or to put on an act.

I am trying to respect him as a being separate from me.
    I am trying not to make him a prisoner,
        not to win him over to my side,
        not to make him follow me.

I am trying to be poor in his sight,
    not to crush him,
        humiliate him,
        or force him to be grateful to me.

I am trying to do these things, Lord, because this man is
unique,
    and he is therefore rich
    with a wealth that I do not possess.
I am the poor one, Lord.

I am standing at his door,
    naked,
    deprived,
    so that, in his heart,
    O risen Christ,
    I may catch a glimpse of your face,
    smiling and inviting me in.

10. My husband is not a Christian

I used to tell myself, 'Once we're married, I'll win him over.'

Well, I tried. At the beginning, I used to urge him, clumsily and too emotionally, to attend mass with me—while pointing out to him that he was free, of course, to do exactly as he wished. He did attend a few services, but he soon grew tired of them. My own zeal eventually diminished, and I settled down into a regular and consoling practice of my religion.

Recently, I was pulled out of my routine by a friend who is a militant Christian. I began to take an active role in religious organisations; and I adopted the practice of reviewing my life in the light of faith. Since that time, I have seen clearly what my duty is to my husband. I must help him discover Jesus (he says that he believes in God) and live in Jesus. But how? I certainly have no intention of going back to the errors and illusions that characterised my earlier, juvenile enthusiasm for his conversion.

A friend of mine who is in the same situation and I have discussed the problem with my parish priest, and, in the light of the Lord, I noted the following.

'Conversion' is a free act. It is free on the part of God, who invites; and free on the part of man, who accepts. It is an encounter between Creator and creature, in personal love.

Human pressure and emotional blackmail retard true conversion, for these things circumscribe freedom and deform the creature.

The initiative is God's in deciding what form his advances

will take. Sometimes he chooses to treat his child none too gently, throwing him to his knees and forcing him suddenly to *see*—without being able to decide where the light is coming from. In general, however, God hides under the appearance of one's neighbour—and this is the approach which he probably uses most in the modern world.

Today, conversion is first of all a conversion to one's neighbour. To be converted means to be 'turned'. It means to go no longer in the direction of self, but in the direction of self-forgetfulness; no longer in the direction of self-interest at the expense of the group, but in that of self-development by the gift of self to the group.

I must search out everything in my husband's life that goes in the direction of the giving of self, in order *to help him enter permanently on that road. In this way, I will be placing him in the path of the Lord.* 'Anyone who claims to be in the light but hates his brother is still in the dark. But anyone who loves his brother is living in the light and need not be afraid of stumbling; unlike the man who hates his brother and is in the darkness, not knowing where he is going, because it is too dark to see' (1 *John* 2: 9–11).

Jesus is present in everyday life, in every opportunity that we have to rise above ourselves. He invites us. I must therefore become a light at my husband's side, so that he does not miss the chance offered by these divine appeals.

It may be that I will never have the joy of hearing the one I love speak Jesus' name clearly. But if he forgets himself totally and faithfully for the sake of an absolute; if he regards service to another as more important than himself—then in a very real way, *he serves his unknown Father and becomes the friend of the Saviour Jesus Christ*, even though he does not know it. It was in this way, in the gospel, that those who were invited to the feast, and knew what was being offered, did not come; but strangers who were available took advantage of the feast.

At the Last Judgement, men will be saved or damned

according to whether or not they give of themselves to another, even though they did not know that it was Jesus to whom they gave or refused themselves.

As a married couple, we are no longer alone. Because of our love, we are two in one flesh. And Jesus has consecrated this love in which God was already present. Through me, and through the sacrament which unites us, my husband attains the true God whom he does not know. I must be the one who, every day, offers to God and consecrates all of our efforts to rise above ourselves at home. In this way, my husband's efforts will also be fulfilled in Christ.

These halting steps of love must find their fulfilment at the sacrifice of the mass. Through Christ's offering, they will achieve their eternal dimension.

I must trust Jesus. I must accept the long, dark night of his love in the life of my husband. I must not ask for 'a sign' to reassure myself or to give me peace of mind. In this way, I will purify my faith and, somehow, help his to germinate.

My husband is redeemed and baptised. He is a son of the Father. Under the hard earth, under the vines and thorns, the seed of faith has been planted. I must work on the basis of that planting and believe that God will never abandon his child.

Lord, I believe in your promise.

Through the sacrament of marriage which we have received and which lives in us, we give the Lord to each other by giving ourselves to each other.

In forgetting myself for the sake of my husband, in loving him, I am giving him God in a much more authentic and certain way than I could by preaching to him even the most moving of sermons.

In loving him, I will help him to love. '. . . Love comes from God and everyone who loves is begotten by God and knows God. Anyone who fails to love can never have known God, because God is love . . . God is love, and anyone who

lives in love lives in God, and God lives in him' (1 *John* 4:
7–8, 16).

And my husband, in loving, will encounter Love.

I'm here, Lord,
     not alone, but with my husband.

You can no longer look at me without seeing him with me,
     for it is you who unite us
          to a far greater degree than we could attain
               through our feeble human love.

Do not let me be tempted to judge him.
Do not let me be tempted to think that I have succeeded.
     For which of us is more adept at loving?
     Only you, who see into our hearts, can tell.

Lord, purify my faith, because it's very hard for me
     to live in darkness, trusting you,
          to love faithfully without asking for a tangible return
          on my love,
          to give you his daily kindnesses so that you may invest
          them,
          to expose the seed of his faith to the sun of your Love.

If it should happen that I never live to rejoice in his visible
     participation in the life of your Church,
If it should happen that our union in you here below will
     never be fulfilled in the light of day,
Then I accept this great sacrifice,
     and I offer it to you,
     so that, in the darkness,
     he may love you more.

11. *The commercial smile and the Christian smile*

The owner of the grocery store where I shop is a good Christian. Although his business prevents him from frequent church-going, he tries to receive communion during the week from time to time. It is also obvious that he tries to live a Christian life. A few days ago, however, he was discouraged. 'This is no business for a man to be in,' he told me. 'I work like a dog—and for next to nothing.' I tried to encourage him, but I can see now that my arguments were all at the human level. Later on, I brought up the subject in our discussion group, and we talked about it in the spirit of faith—the role of the businessman and also our role as consumers. We were astonished at what we turned up.

I wonder now whether I'll have enough humility and enough faith to be able to help my grocer reconsider his life in relation to his trade.

All human work is a participation in the great Christian mystery of the creation. Together, each of us in our place, we are completing the universe; and no one has the right to withdraw from that providential task.

The role of our grocer is to feed other men. He makes it possible for them to live and to grow.

All human work is also a service rendered by men to other men. In the case of a grocer, the service is rendered directly.

Thus, a tradesman should not try to sell only the most expensive items. He should try to 'serve' his customers to the best of his ability by selling them what they actually need.

He must think of others before he thinks of the cash register.

A businessman who deceives his customers, who creates artificial needs by exaggerated advertising, is a thief and an oppressor of mankind. He is not serving humanity. Taken as a whole, this kind of businessman, when joined to all the others who look only for profit, is building that 'consumer society' which alienates man and forces innumerable young people into despair, revolt or escape.

Work is not a one-way street. It is an exchange of services. My grocer sells vegetables, cheese, fruit and so forth, to feed us. We give him money—which he exchanges for shoes, clothing, housing.

We must therefore change our attitude towards tradesmen. For it is proud, unreasonable and out of place: 'I pay; therefore I should be thanked.' Instead, *we should thank one another*.

Through the daily exchange of services, God offers to businessmen and their customers a heaven-sent opportunity to tighten the bonds between men, and to strengthen that human unity for which Jesus died. It is the particular responsibility of Christians to channel Jesus' love into these natural relationships.

Everything that works for greater attention to persons opens the way to the Lord. For customers, this means simple things, like not wanting half-a-pound of butter to be split, and trying to do one's shopping at the least busy times of the day.

In retail selling as in many other professions, the exchange often goes far beyond mere objects. There are human contacts, handshakes, smiles, words and the marvellous gift of a moment of real attention.

We must replace the 'commercial smile' with a Christian smile. Jesus needs the grocer so that every day he may serve his brothers and give them—as Jesus himself did—bread and fish, and also infinite love.

Business makes it possible to create ties not only at the level of distributors and buyers, but also at the level of those who are in the same business.

Business should be organised and practised so as *to give better service* to customers and to allow businessmen to live honestly and honourably. In this sense, such things as quantity-buying, middle-men, distribution, price-fixing, price-control and taxes, all pertain to charity and therefore to the mystery of Christ.

Work should allow the worker to develop. It should not make him less a man, or crush him. It should pay him a living wage, obviously; but it should also offer him the opportunity to fulfil himself by giving of himself, by allowing him to seek just treatment, and by giving him responsibility.

To belong to professional organisations and participate in them is therefore—here as elsewhere—to work with the Lord in building the Kingdom of the Father in and through human reality.

Work is not a punishment. It is an honour, and a great honour, conferred on man by God the Creator; but, *because of sin, work has become a burden*. That is one of the consequences of sin.

None the less, Jesus Christ came down on earth to give meaning to work, as to all suffering. What was useless before his coming, the spoiled fruit of human selfishness, is now an opportunity for salvation. We participate in the Redemption, not by enduring the pain of work, but by bearing it and offering it to Jesus.

Once a businessman commits himself to the struggle for the best possible management of his profession, all that is painful in his life as a businessman becomes, if he is a Christian, an opportunity for redemption—the demands of his customers, fatigue, pressure, uncertain business conditions, the effort it takes for him to be pleasant.

The opportunity we have to participate in the Redemption

comes to us in our daily lives. And, for every one of us, the Way of the Cross may be found along the road of our working lives.

We all have 'vocations'. We are called by God to be sellers or buyers, merchants or consumers. Jesus waits for us in our work, as he waits for us in all other aspects of our activity. At the price of our entire lives, we share holiness with him.

Lord, tonight I am thinking about all the businessmen in this city.
>I am thinking about your great confidence in the men whom you have judged worthy of working together to continue your creation.
>I am thinking of the opportunities for mutual service which you offer every day to millions of persons.
>I am thinking of your silent invitation
>>to tighten those mysterious bonds which,
>>>out of diverse members,
>>>will build your great Body.

Lord, forgive us for all the twisted roads
>and the dead-end streets
>built by the servants of the great god, profit;
>>for these deform creation,
>>by exploiting their brothers.

Forgive those who buy
>in order to build an artificial paradise
>and to enjoy it as an end in itself.

Teach us to do our shopping
>as Mary, your mother, did hers,
>and as you yourself, as a child,
>>did when you took her place.

Make us grateful for the services rendered
>by trades people.

Make us, by our greeting, pay attention first to the person who is selling, rather than to the objects we are buying.

The Kingdom of Heaven is like unto a businessman . . .
The Kingdom of Heaven is like unto a housewife . . .

Lord, why do I go far afield looking for your love?
    You are waiting for me, every day,
    to distribute to men their daily bread,
    or to accompany me while I do my shopping.

12. There is someone among you you don't even know

Every year we condemn in the severest terms the pagan manifestations surrounding the religious feast of Christmas. We are shocked and disgusted by everything, from the outrageous expenditures for gifts to the forced 'good cheer', from the exaggerated emotions of midnight mass to the smell of stuffed turkey.

All of our brothers stand before our court of judgement, non-Christians as well as those who, as we say, 'call themselves Christians'. As always, we are among the judges rather than among the accused. And behind our self-righteous judgements there lurks something worse, the attitude of Pharisees. We, thank God, are not like the rest of men. For us, Christmas is God, the true God of Christians who, in Christ Jesus, has come to save us.

It is no doubt true that people mutilate and caricature the Christmas message. But what right have we to judge their intentions and pass sentence on them? And why do we insist on seeing only the negative side of these festivities? Through the eyes of faith, it is just as easy to see in these simple emotions and efforts at merry-making an unconscious appeal to the God of love who has come down among men. We should try to accept, as an opportunity for conversion, this boisterous celebration of Jesus' birthday which the Church, in its liturgy, encourages us to re-live. Is our love so pure that we can afford to dispense with such things? Do we not also tend to strip God of his true nature? Do we not also set up 'graven images'—even idols? Wouldn't the prophet be

71

justified in saying to us, as well as to others: 'There is one among you whom you do not know.'

Too often, people think of God
> as a common name which has become part of everyday language;
> as a vague 'being' who is supposed to have magical powers;
> as the creative force behind the universe and its evolution;
> as an idea which can be demonstrated in order to comfort the minds of men.
>> But this is not the God of the Christians.

Too often, and for too many people, the 'act of faith' is summed up in this manner: There is 'something' greater than us, something inapproachable because it is so distant, unknowable because it is mysterious; something which we must contend with and endure; something we must try to bend to our own will; something whose good will we must cultivate.
> This is in no way the faith of Christians.

Too often men speak of 'being religious' or of 'having religion'. They refer to a complex
> of badly assimilated religious information,
> of badly observed moral laws,
> of rituals, often idolatrous in themselves, performed distractedly,
> of social concepts which are as ultra-conservative for some as they are revolutionary for others.
>> This is by no means the religion of Christians.

The God of the Christians is not
> a god-object,
> a god-idea,
> a god of morality,
> a god of social order.

The God of the Christians is

a *person*,
a person who is called Jesus Christ;
a person who, historically, once lived among men.
The God of the Christians is not
'something' greater than us, but
someone among us.

Christmas, then, is God come among us, made visible to us.

Christmas is God, hitherto inaccessible and unknown, becoming man and joining hands with men, greeting men, speaking to men, loving men, dying for men. 'No one has ever seen God; it is only the Son, who is nearest to the Father's heart, who has made him known' (*John* 1: 18). 'The Word was made flesh, he lived among us, and we saw his glory' (*John* 1: 14).

St John was still caught up in the excitement of that encounter when he wrote: 'Something which has existed since the beginning, that we have heard, and we have seen with our own eyes; that we have watched and touched with our hands: the Word, who is life--this is our subject. That life was made visible: we saw it and we are giving our testimony, telling you of eternal life which was with the Father and has been made visible to us. What we have seen and heard we are telling you so that you too may be in union with us, as we are in union with the Father and with his Son Jesus Christ. We are writing this to you to make our own joy complete' (1 *John* 1: 1–4).

God became man for the whole of mankind, and therefore for me. He came to see me, to speak to me, to become my friend, to save me. *I am personally involved with him.*

Many men are deists. They believe in a Creator-God who imposes order on the universe.

Christians, however, *believe in Jesus Christ*, trust in him, live with him and in him within his Church, and work for the Kingdom of his Father.

73

Some Christians are badly in need of being re-educated. In extreme cases, they are capable of knowing and practising their religion 'sociologically', without knowing their God. What they need is to find Jesus Christ, who is the source and the life. 'This is the testimony: God has given us eternal life and this life is in his Son; anyone who has the Son has life, anyone who does not have the Son does not have life' (1 *John* 5: 11–12). And 'if anyone acknowledges that Jesus is the Son of God, God lives in him, and he in God' (1 *John* 4: 15).

Why are we Christians rather than Buddhists, say, or Moslems? Because we have confidence in Jesus Christ and not in Buddha or Mohammed. Why do we belong to the Catholic Church rather than to another Church? Because *it was Jesus Christ who founded this Church, and only this Church.* We may suffer from the imperfections of the Church's human face, but we recognise that we are part of that Church. We will never agree to the establishment of another Church alongside our Church; but we work, none the less, to purify the Church when we purify ourselves, so that Jesus' plan for it may be realised in an ever more perfect way.

It is very hard for us to recognise the profound reality of Jesus Christ under the visible signs of the Church, even when those signs are the sacraments themselves.

We tend to think of grace as 'something that we receive'. We say: 'I'll ask God for grace'—whereas grace is, in fact, Christ's life in us, his love which saves us and transforms us in the very root of our being.

God became man so that man could become god; that is, so that man could be 'divinised' in Jesus Christ. In this sense, the Christian's act of faith is not: 'I believe that God exists.' It is not even: 'I believe in a personal God, someone who has come among men.' It is this: 'I believe in Jesus Christ, who loves me and saves me.'

For a Christian, to believe means to accept being loved

infinitely, being forgiven, being saved. The Christian's God is not someone who must be appeased, or, even primarily someone who must be loved. His God is above all someone by whom he must allow himself to be loved. The greatness of the Christian's God is not that he is all-powerful, but that he is all-loving. His transcendence is the absolute of love, not the absolute of philosophers.

'God's love for us was revealed when God sent into the world his only Son, so that we could have life through him; this is the love I mean: not our love for God, but God's love for us when he sent his Son to be the sacrifice that takes our sins away' (1 *John* 4: 9–10).

'We ourselves have known and put our faith in God's love toward ourselves. *God is love* and anyone who lives in love lives in God, and God lives in him' (1 *John* 4: 16).

I am loved by God, since the beginning of time, infinitely.

That I am a sinner does not keep God from loving me. Holiness does not consist in being without sin. On the contrary, it means acknowledging that *I am a sinner* (and not merely that I am someone who commits sins), accepting that fact within myself, and believing with all my strength that Jesus loves me just as I am and *that his love saves me*. This is what Jesus meant when he said, 'I did not come to call the virtuous, but sinners' (*Matt.* 9: 12).

'The word was made flesh.'

'There is someone among you whom you do not know.'

He is called Love.

Lord, forgive me for having mutilated your Face, as vandals rip and tear at a priceless work of art.

Forgive me for having mistaken you for a mere subject of discussion, as though faith were the result of a demonstration.[1]

1. Faith is not irrational. It is reasonable to believe in Jesus, but reason cannot make us believe in Jesus Christ, the Son of God and the Saviour of

Forgive me for having used you as a tranquilliser for my restless mind, as though you were the inaccessible god of the philosophers.

Forgive me for having used you as a 'spiritual weapon' against the 'spirit of materialism', as though human salvation were a campaign rather than the mystery of Jesus, dead and risen.

When I discovered that you were a person, Lord, and that you were nearby, I did not act accordingly.
Forgive me for having too often acted as though:
> You were someone who had come to pay a bill;
> You were someone whose commandments I had to follow in order to be in your good graces and to have the right to eternal life;
> You were someone rich and powerful from whom, through prayer, I could obtain favours.

Lord, I forgot the most important thing; the essential thing, without which the rest is nothing, or, at best, a ridiculous caricature.
I forgot, God, that you are an infinitely loving Father and that it has been your eternal plan to make me your son.
I forgot, God, that you are Love,
> and that Love has come down among us.
> > I forgot, God, to let myself be loved.

Mankind. Only grace can do that. 'No one can come to me unless he is drawn by the Father who sent me' (*John* 6: 44).

13. There are too many people we just leave asleep

Going over some of my notes last night, I came across this sentence of Saint-Exupéry's which I had written down some time in the past: 'There are too many people we just leave asleep.' It was there, in my handwriting, on the back of an old envelope. The Lord, in the twinkling of an eye (as he so often does), had given me a sign. I meditated in his light and did a rapid reappraisal of my life. Rather than judge those who sleep, and become discouraged over how many of them there are, I should try to wake them up and help them to grow. How many times will Jesus have to remind me of it?

We are surrounded by people. Among them, there are some who are struggling to grow, to go beyond themselves, to fight alongside their brothers for justice, human dignity and peace. Among Christians, there are a few of these militants—so few, perhaps, that we can count them on the fingers of one hand.

Men exist as though life were a train roaring through the night. Made drowsy by the movement of the train, they sleep, and they are carried along. They were placed on the train. Do they know where they are going? Do they know why they are travelling? Will they wake up even when they reach their station?

It is terribly tempting to be discouraged when we meet someone who neither hungers nor thirsts—someone we know at work; a neighbour in another flat in our block; one of our friends. There is a multitude of people who are satisfied with themselves, whose stomachs are full, so to speak, and who are not interested in growing or in fighting for others. 'We have enough to live on,' they say. 'We'll get by'—as though man could 'get by' in eternal life!—'and, so far as the others are concerned, let them take care of themselves.'

And yet, in our bodies, our hearts, our minds, we have been created to grow. We are designed for action. It is up to us to build the world, and all men are invited to participate actively in the human groups to which they belong.

Mankind itself, as a whole, must continue to progress in time. We must take part in that ascending spiral: our sons must be greater than we are, and their sons must be greater than they. God wants us to grow. Like any father, he cannot bear to see his sons become weaklings or cripples, either in body or in mind. All men are called to be perfect, as their Father in heaven is perfect. All human groups are called to become a community in Christ.

Regardless of appearances, we should not judge others, for
    people who appear to be sleeping may actually be
        meditating;
    people who appear to be unenthusiastic may actually be
        under strict self-control;
    people who appear to be children may be wise old men.
Regardless of appearances, we cannot judge others since we do not know
    what they have had to put up with,
    what they have tried to do,
    what has happened to them.

No matter how lacking in energy those around us may be, we must not be discouraged. For if a man sleeps, he is sleeping on a treasure: a hidden treasure which he may have buried, or one the existence of which he ignores—but one which, none the less, must be discovered, unearthed, revealed.

The human potential for development, for the giving of oneself and for human solidarity, can never be exhausted; for man is its source, and he is an infinite source. He has his origins in the eternal thought of God. Before the universe was created, man existed in God, in his love from all eternity.

Man is infinitely greater, more precious and more fertile than he thinks. When we have faith, it is impossible to despair of man. To do so would be an injustice to God. But there are men around us to whom no one will ever render the service of releasing their captive energies, their inexhaustible riches, their potential for commitment.

If there are men around us who are sleeping, it is because we ourselves are not sufficiently awake. We live with our eyes half closed, or looking up at the sky, or—more often—fixed on ourselves; and so we walk through life without seeing the wounded and sleeping men by the roadside.

The hidden riches of a man are those of life, love and the ability to give of himself. *We reveal these riches to him when we give him the opportunity to make use of them.*

We must pay attention to other people, listen to them, so that we may ask them,
>   at the proper time,
>   in the proper place,
>   for the service, however small, that they can render.

When we waken a sleeping man so that he may serve his brothers, we must often ask him
>   first, to give something to his brothers;
>   then, to give them something more;
>   later, to give them something of his own—his time, for example;
>   finally, we must help him *to give himself.*

One day, this wakened man will stand astonished before the treasure which has been revealed to him, and he will say:

'I had no idea that I was capable of doing such things for other people.' At that moment, he is saved. Having begun to give, he will have begun to grow.

Such a man rediscovers the interior source of growth, and he is consciously in contact with it as it pours forth its energy. Soon, he will be able to give it a name; for that source in him is infinite love: God.

Jesus, always mindful of others, said first of all to the Samaritan woman, 'Give me a drink.' And, because he awakened in her the source of giving, despite the obstacle of sin, she became capable of receiving the supreme revelation: ' "Whoever drinks this water will get thirsty again; but anyone who drinks the water that I shall give will never be thirsty again: the water that I shall give will turn into a spring inside him, welling up to eternal life." The woman said to him, "I know that Messiah—that is, Christ—is coming" . . . "I who am speaking to you," said Jesus, "I am he" ' (*John* 4: 13–14, 25–26).

Lord, tonight I ask you to forgive us for all the men whose development has been arrested:
> for the dwarfs, the weaklings, the deformed, the handicapped,
> for all those aborted beings who have disappointed your paternal love.

I ask forgiveness for all those who sleep, or who are so paralysed, frustrated, self-centred, indifferent, discouraged and disgusted
> that they no longer try to grow,
> that they no longer know how to grow,
> that they no longer want to grow,
and who therefore put down their arms and withdraw,
> leaving their brothers to fight alone.

Above all, Lord, I ask your forgiveness for myself.

I've passed by these wounded, captive ones
    without seeing them,
      or without going to them: 'He saw him, and con-
      tinued on his way.'
I did not offer them the opportunity
    to awaken,
    to begin to live again,
    to rejoin their brothers in battle.

Lord, let me sit each day at the side of the well,
    tired, perhaps, but still alert.
Let me be the one who asks passers-by.
    for myself and my brothers:
    'Give me a drink.'

Forgive us, Lord, for 'there are too many people whom we just leave asleep'.

14. Our little girl is a young woman

I had prepared her for this. In order to do a good job of it, I had also prepared myself by searching, in the light of faith, for the deepest meaning of this important step in the physical and psychological development of my daughter.

When Jacqueline came to me and happily told me what had happened, I kissed her. And then, together, we improvised a prayer to thank God for his goodness to her. There was now in her a source of life, hidden but none the less real. Together, we went to tell her father the news. He gave her the small gift that we had selected some time before; and he told her that, from that time on, she would choose her own clothes. I would go with her, we explained, to make sure that her choice was not too expensive; but I would respect her tastes (which, I confess, won't be an easy thing to do).

At dinner that night, we had a little celebration, and we took the opportunity afterwards to explain things to her brother. We must make sure that he has a sufficient appreciation of feminine dignity so that, now and later, he will treat women with proper respect.

To be frank, I couldn't help envying my daughter a little. In spite of myself, I thought; 'She's so lucky to have parents like us.' I remembered my own childhood and the shame and guilt I experienced when I began to mature. But then, I thanked God for allowing us to live, at least a little, in the faith. All that God has made is good, and how stupid we are to drag down to our human level and to deform and corrupt what God intends to be great and beautiful.

The entry into adolescence by a girl or boy is a sign from God, made through the intermediary of the laws of nature, that he has conferred on them an extraordinary dignity. He has made them capable of co-creating other men with him.

This mission was given to man at the time of his creation: 'Be fruitful, multiply, fill the earth.' It is the noblest mission assigned by God to his sons, for when they accomplish it in love, they most resemble the Almighty. Like him and with him, they are creators.

Every man must give life, either physically or spiritually. A life which does not bear fruit is a failure.

Physical development is the sign, in the flesh, of God's eternal plan for man.

A child is worthy of infinite respect because he is innocence itself. The adolescent is worthy of the same respect because he is a promise of what is to come.

An adolescent is not conscious of his dignity. It must be revealed to him. He is vulnerable, and we must help him because he is weak and uneasy. He has, after all, just become a repository of life.

This life came to him from the very source of life, from the hands of God. It contains in itself the life of his parents, and through it they live in him. This spark of life moves, burns, demands to be passed on.

To carry this marvellous source within themselves confers a great dignity of young men and women; but it also entails a great responsibility.

So far as the parents are concerned, this essential step by their child towards maturity is an invitation from God to purify their love. He reminds them that, although they have 'given' life, it is not theirs to hold on to. They must let it go, so that it, too, may give life. 'A man leaves his father and his mother to cleave to his wife . . .'

A child is entirely in the hands of its parents: body, heart and mind.

The adolescent must gradually receive, from their hands, sole responsibility for himself. For the young man must possess his entire self if he is to be able one day to give himself to others.

The body of an adolescent no longer belongs to his parents. It belongs to him. The parents must accept the fact that their child wants less and less attention from them for his body. They must, none the less, help the adolescent develop that body in a healthy and balanced manner. They must clothe it, care for it, respect it and ensure that it is respected by others. In other words, they must prepare their child for the day on which he will be totally on his own.

The heart of the adolescent belongs not to his parents, but to himself. The parents must accept that their child has less and less need for their presence and for the expression of their affection. They must, however, help him learn to love truly in friendship and in the giving of self to others. They must prepare him for the day on which his heart is wholly his own.

The mind of the adolescent belongs not to his parents, but to himself. The parents must accept the fact that their child no longer wishes to follow them blindly in their ideas, their tastes, their choices. But they must help him to think for himself, to form his own opinions, to develop his own tastes, to establish his own motivations. They must prepare him for the day on which he will be a truly mature adult.

The life of the adolescent belongs not to his parents, but to himself. The parents must recognise that their child wishes gradually to free himself from the obligation of purely passive obedience. They must help him to make decisions for himself, judge for himself, act for himself. For soon, he will be ready to exercise his full freedom as a man.

It is difficult to love, because to love is to renounce oneself for the sake of another. And self-renunciation is always very painful.

When a child comes into the world, it detaches itself

84

from the body of its mother; and the mother bleeds. When an adult comes into the world, he must likewise detach himself from his parents; and the parents will bleed in their hearts. 'You shall give birth to your children in pain.'

The greatness of man consists in his ability to create himself.

The success of a teacher consists in being able to say, 'My students no longer need me.'

The grandeur of parents consists in their having propagated the life which they carried in themselves. Their mission is to transmit that life, and to withdraw gradually when they see it begin to bloom in their children. For their children, in their turn, must 'be fruitful, multiply, fill the earth'.

How unhappy they are who, through selfishness, interrupt or break the cycle of life.

Prayer of a young woman, inspired by her mother

Thank you, Lord, for having let life develop in me.

Let me receive this marvellous gift with pride and respect.
Let me be strong and generous enough,
 to care for my body,
 to develop it,
 and to respect it,
 so that it may be a worthy receptacle of life.
Let this life, through me, spread and bloom in joy for
 all those around me who are wasting away or dying.

Lord, I pray for my parents.
Help them to say goodbye to their little girl, and help them welcome the young woman, who is their daughter, with pride and joy.
Let them have enough love and generosity to tend what another will reap.

Let them never resent the one who will one day take me away,

> but let them forget themselves so that they may prepare to give me away.

Help me to be gentle with them so that their suffering may be lessened, and their sacrifice, through me, may bear the fruits of happiness.

I also pray, Lord,

> for all those adolescents who are unaware of their dignity,
> for all the young women who resent or regret their feminity,
> and for those who misuse, waste and pervert what you have given them with such love.

Let this life in my body, if you wish it, Lord, be one day a sparkling spring.

Let it meet another spring; and let the waters mix, and bring forth another life.

Let me remain yours, Lord, and let me be ever grateful to you; for you have 'done great things for me'.

15. A miracle tranquilliser

At work this morning, Jack told me that his doctor had ordered him to stay at home for several weeks. It seems he was suffering from nervous depression.

One of the women in the flat next-door to us has been constantly complaining to my wife that she 'doesn't sleep a wink all night'. Her doctor has given her some sleeping pills.

Another friend of my wife's is on tranquillisers.

As for myself, my nerves are in a bad way. My doctor has limited me to one cup of coffee a day and told me to cut down my smoking.

We are not alone, of course. All around us, people are overwrought, tense, restless. They are all looking for a less hectic way of life; and, even more, they are looking for a miracle drug to relax them, tranquillise them, make them sleep.

I wonder if we are going about this in the right way. I suspect that there is another way to save men who are tormented, torn and bruised, and who are at the point of collapse. Surely the Lord has something to say to us in the midst of our agony—an effective tranquilliser of his own to propose.

There is a sudden crack in the living-room wall. The owner of the house is frightened. He covers the crack with expensive wallpaper. For the moment, he feels better. He is tranquillised.

But the crack widens and tears the paper. The man covers

the crack with a thicker paper, and again he is tranquillised.

It may seem ridiculous, but man follows the same pattern in other areas of his life. He closes his eyes when he sees a problem, and, for the moment, he feels better. But the problem remains.

Human remedies very often cure symptoms, rather than diseases. They do not go to the heart of the problem.

Certainly, modern man must have the courage to try to find peace, relaxation, sleep. Certainly, he must fight with all his strength for better living conditions. But are the sound and the fury all *outside* man? Does the pressure come only from work and from traffic jams? Isn't it also within man himself? Is there tension only in life, or does it exist also in the human heart?

Man today exists in a piecemeal fashion. Overwhelmed as he is by outside commitments, he ends up by exploding. His vitality, his sexuality, his emotions, his imagination—all of his faculties—are drifting away from the essential unity of his personality.

What really exhausts modern man is the perpetual search for his 'identity'. His overworked and over-extended faculties pull him in every direction until he is hardly conscious of what he is doing. His nervous system at first puts up with this gruelling pace; then, one day, it too is exhausted, and collapses.

In the face of this crisis, some men say that this is real and total freedom; that man must allow all of his strength to be brought into play so that he may fulfil himself at his own pace. Others, by an act of the will, impose a certain interior discipline upon themselves, and succeed only in deforming and perverting their frustrated faculties.

Some men appeal to taboos, to moral laws—but without bothering about where these taboos and laws come from. And other men run to their doctors and psychiatrists, or take refuge in drugs which give them the illusion of peace.

It is the Christian belief that there is a flaw within man which existed long before this internal rift, and which goes much deeper than the latter. Human nature itself has been wounded by sin—that is, by non-love. Man's various faculties are trying to fulfil themselves individually, independently of one another, without reference to any hierarchy of values or to any objective except their own individual satisfaction. The external irritations provided by the modern world work towards this imbalance and aggravate it.

At the same time, there exists in man a deep desire for interior harmony, for peace and the development of his entire being. Every man is destined to achieve the supreme success: divinisation. At the very beginning, it was suggested to man that he strike out on his own. 'You will be like gods,' he was told—gods without God.

Man, however, is only a draft, a rough copy. Alone, he is incapable of attaining his full stature. It is only in Jesus Christ, the Saviour, that we can be made divine: 'Before the world was made, he chose us, chose us in Christ . . . determining that we should become his adopted sons, through Jesus Christ' (*Eph.* 1: 4–5).

We are therefore on the horns of a dilemma. Man must either try to fulfil himself by his own efforts, without God, and thus surrender to interior anarchy; or he must be willing to open himself to God's saving Love and become, at every moment of his life, the *new man*, unified and at peace with himself (but not necessarily free from suffering). St Paul understood this and expressed it perfectly: to live, he said, is Christ.

The cause of modern man's crisis is that he does not know God and wants to do without him. But the farther away he gets from God, and the more he makes use of human tranquillisers, the greater harm he does to himself. His final punishment, if he does not discover Christ the Saviour, will be that *he will destroy himself from within*.

Since we not only commit sins but also and above all are

essentially sinners—that is, sinful in our very natures—we must freely place Christ the Saviour at the centre of our being. He will then re-establish unity within us and give us peace.

The sacrament of penance is no longer fashionable. Yet, whatever its exterior form, it is indispensable to the modern world, for it offers redemption to each of us, and the opportunity to reduce the sins which tear us apart. We are saved by Love, which re-establishes harmony and order in our being and gives us profound peace. 'Peace I bequeath to you,' Jesus said, 'my own peace I give you, *a peace the world cannot give*, this is my gift to you' (*John* 14: 27).

We must ask Jesus to save us, but we must also offer ourselves to him. Every man, whatever his life may be, and whatever kind of world he lives in, can gather himself up—that is, collect the whole of his faculties—and reassemble himself so as to begin the journey towards other men and towards God. And, if he wishes to live, he *must* do so.

It takes only a few seconds, anywhere, at any time, to give *all*. For it is our life, whole and entire, that we must place in God's hands.

'I seek Yahweh, and he answers me,
　　and frees me from all my fears' (*Ps.* 34: 4).

'In God alone there is rest for my soul,
　　from him comes my safety' (*Ps.* 62: 1).

'My eyes are always on Yahweh,
　　for he releases my feet from the net' (*Ps.* 25: 15).

'Unload your burden on to Yahweh,
　　and he will support you;
he will never permit
　　the virtuous to falter' (*Ps.* 55: 22).

'I keep Yahweh before me always,
for with him at my right hand nothing can shake me.
So my heart exults, my very soul rejoices,
my body, too, will rest securely' (*Ps.* 16: 8–9).

'In peace I lie down, and fall asleep at once,
since you alone, Yahweh, make me rest secure' (*Ps.* 4: 8).

   'He provides for his beloved as they sleep' (*Ps.* 127: 2).

16. Houses for the children of God

My friend Peter is active in a tenants' association. 'I live on the sixth floor of a big block of flats,' he explained, 'in a district where there are many large buildings. From my window at night, I can see hundreds of other lighted windows. I imagine that, behind each one of them, there are families—people who, later, will try to sleep in order to recover their energy. I sometimes think of the thousands—no, the millions—of other men who, at that moment, are reaching their homes—or at least reaching what serves them as home. I meditate, with God, on the problem of housing. Is the Lord interested in housing? And, as a Christian, have I other reasons for worrying about it than to be of help to my fellow men?'

A tree needs to be planted in the earth in order to take root, to grow and bear fruit. A man and his family likewise need a home in order to live and to grow.

The more a man is taken away from home by his work or other activities, the more he is internally preoccupied by his many obligations and distracted by outside demands on his time, then the more he needs a home to which he can withdraw, and where he can relax and rebuild his strength.

A man's house is the primary place where he can find recreation—where he can rest, read, eat, sleep—and where, as a son of God, he can regain his strength through prayer.

What is true for a man is also true for his family. The more a family is scattered by their various daily activities, the more it requires a place to which it can return and in which it can be reunited.

When men and women are obliged to leave their homes—for work, for example—society, for better or worse, provides various substitute 'centres': youth centres, for example, or child-care centres. When children become 'problem' or 'maladjusted' or 'delinquent' because of the absence of their parents, society tries to repair the damage by means of such centres. Advanced as such centres may be, there is nothing new in the idea behind them. They aim at nothing more than the establishment of artificial families, by such means as grouping together the children from one district or one building.

The Lord has said that man should not pull asunder what God has joined together. But what has God joined together? Husband and wife, of course. But also the entire family unit: father, mother, children, all are bound together in love and by love and are thus a living reflection of the Trinity.

The most noble aspect of the human vocation is to be, with God, a creator; and it is in his home, in the midst of his family, that a man fulfils that vocation. In exercising that responsibility, with love, he corresponds most closely to the image of God.

In this sense, every home is a temple:
a temple for the sons of God,
a temple for the members of the family who are images of the Trinity.

If our faith were truly alive and the ceremony of blessing houses had not lost all significance, it would therefore be perfectly logical to consecrate homes as we consecrate churches.

Every man and every family have a right to decent housing. No one can rest while there are millions who lack it.

A man who owns an empty house or flat and, without good reason, allows it to remain empty, is guilty before his brothers and before God.

A man who says 'I love God' because he contributes to the building of a church, and yet is not *at least concerned* with housing problems, is either a fool or a liar. No gift, no matter how generous and legitimate it may be, made for the service of God or of the Christian community, can free a Christian of his obligation also to serve his fellow man.

It is a grave error, if not a sin, for a man to allow or encourage luxury in the churches and in the houses of God's children so long as there are millions of men who have no worthy place to lay their heads. When a Christian speaks of glorifying God, he must mean, first of all, preserving the dignity of God's children. Therefore, what a man has over and beyond his needs does not belong to him but to his brothers.

Since the essential function of a home is to allow a man to rest and to allow a family to create and to grow in love, anything which facilitates that function is in conformity with what God asks of us:

A home for every family (the family being the basic unit of mankind); a common room where the family may meet together; sufficient comfort for the body to free the mind; sufficient privacy (sound-insulation, for example) to allow a man to think, and other such things in line with human needs and human dignity.

It is up to man to develop the necessary technology for these things. It is up to the Christian to guide that development in the light of faith; for faith alone gives meaning to any human enterprise.

Such an undertaking is the work of many men: the architect who designs buildings; the institute of standards which determines the strength of materials; the contractors, masons, carpenters and plumbers; the statesmen who work

out the problems of housing, the legislators who allocate
funds for building, and the tenants' associations which
work to establish and defend their rights. They, and many
more, all work, each in his proper place, at an undertaking
which is far beyond their own means. For they are not only
building houses for men; they are building temples for the
children of God.

Lord, tonight I'm talking to you in my house.
Around me, other men are in their own houses.
> But there are also many men crowded together in slums
> and shacks;
> and many more, throughout the world, who must
> sleep on the bare ground, exposed to the elements.

While I pray, there are others praying;
> some are eating their daily bread,
> some are sleeping,
> some are loving,
>> as you have told them to do.

Some men, however, are quarrelling,
> and some are fighting among themselves.
Some run away because they can bear no more,
> and some refuse life because there is no more room for
> children.
Some even lose their minds because the noise keeps them
from sleeping.
> I know this is not what you want.
The housing of men is important, Lord.
Perhaps it is more important today than it was yesterday,
> because man today, exhausted as he is and worn out
> by the pace of life,
> has a greater need of rest;
> because man today, with more education and
> experience,

has a greater need to recover his interior unity;
because the family today is more immediately face to
face with its creative responsibilities.

Lord, you've told us that when we give shelter to a man,
we give shelter to you.
It's very disturbing when you identify everyone with yourself.
It's not practical, because then we can't get away from you,
and we find you everywhere in our lives.
Even when we give to your Church you don't dispense us
from providing you with a decent home.
You tell us instead that we must do the same
for those with whom you identify yourself:
'I was without shelter . . .' you said.

Father, help us so that your children
no longer have to be born in stables or caves.
Help us so that they may grow and develop,
physically, intellectually and spiritually,
as you wish them to.
Help us so that your great Human Body may take shape.
Help us to build houses for men.
Help me personally to take part in this work,
even if it is only to contribute a word to a discussion,
or to put a ballot into a box,
or perhaps to do even more, if you wish it,
so that, henceforth, there will be room for all your children
in the inns of the world.

17. In the image of God

I asked Jack to come to union headquarters tonight to help me run off some circulars. I could do it alone, but we're trying to get him involved. It's a little thing, and the kind of thing I could do for many of the other people at work. Why am I doing it?

I think I've made some progress. It's because I've tried, not to take the place of others, but to help them take their own proper place; because I've tried discreetly to edge others towards opportunities to become involved at their own level. It's become almost a habit for me to try to get the people around me to give of themselves. That's why I wonder whether it hasn't become almost too automatic—whether it isn't a refined 'apostolic technique' rather than a gesture full of meaning, love and faith. Today, I must go back to the basic reasons for my actions. I must examine, in the light of faith, the motives for what I do.

I've read a few paragraphs of an article on God. In them, I discovered something that had never occurred to me. The Lord spoke to me through his doctrine, lighting up my life at the very moment when I was about to forget to join myself to him in faith.

God is not alone. If he were, he would be incredibly self-centred. But he is three persons—three persons so intimately united that they are one God.

To love means to forget oneself entirely for the sake of another. It means to give oneself totally and freely in order to enrich another and to become one with him.

In the Trinity, each of the three persons tends wholly towards the others. Each of them is wholly a relationship with respect to the others—a 'subsistent relationship', the theologians call it. It is in that sense that God 'is' love.

'All I have is yours and all you have is mine' (*John* 17: 10).
'The Father and I are one' (*John* 10: 30).
'You will know for sure that the Father is in me and I am in the Father' (*John* 10: 38).

> Each person in the Trinity is
> total giving,
> total relationship,
> total love.

To put it in human terms, we might say that if the persons of the Trinity ceased to love, they would cease to exist.

Now, God has created man in his image—which means, among other things, that he created man in such a way as to be able to give himself and to exist in relationship to his brothers. Thus, man can fulfil himself only in giving himself and in loving through individual and collective relationships.

We should become what we are. We should release the image of God that is within us; we should perfect it little by little as the sculptor gradually draws from his marble the design which he has conceived.

Man can 'be' only by forgetting himself entirely in order to tend wholly towards others.

Man can 'be' only by being wholly *a relationship with others*. Therefore, the quality of his relationships is the measure of the depth and the development of his being.

> The more I forget myself to give myself to others,
> the more I lose myself to find others,
> the more I release myself to reach out to others,

then the more I become the image of God and the more
I 'am' a person, as God intended me to be
'Anyone who loves his life loses it; anyone who hates his
life in this world will keep it for the eternal life' (*John* 12:
25).

All that tends towards others is life.
All that tends towards myself is death.

When I help others to forget themselves in order to give
themselves, I am helping them to develop the image of God
in them. I am helping them to 'be'.

There are no 'little things' when it comes to giving.
The smallest gesture towards others, even at the purely
material level, is a step forward in the development of
one's being. We learn to give by giving.

If we have the opportunity to give in our everyday lives,
it is because the Lord offers such opportunities so that we
may grow.

When I am asked

not to do something, but to make someone else do
something;

not to give, but to help someone else to give;

not to establish a personal relationship with someone,
but to help someone else to establish relationships in the
natural groups to which he belongs,

it is in order to take him out of himself and help him
become a man—a man such as God has planned from
all eternity.

'This is my commandment: love one another as I have
loved you' (*John* 15: 12).

'May they all be one. Father, may they be one in us, as
you are in me and I am in you' (*John* 17: 21).

Jesus has given us his life in order to raise our giving and
our loving to the level of Trinitarian love. We must truly
become not only the *image* of God, but divinised persons.

We must become not only the body known as 'humanity'
but the Body of Christ.

Who am I, lord?
Why am I dissatisfied?
Why do I feel as though I am on a journey, always moving?
Why do I feel I'm not whole, stable, certain, secure,
    so that I want to feel sure of myself and not have to
    struggle?
There is in me the image of God which I must freely perfect.
bit by bit, in the midst of my daily life.
I am in the process of becoming;
    and so are those around me,
    and all of mankind as it moves painfully towards unity.

I worship you, God, who are pure gift,
                        pure love.
I know you as my all and as my end.
Let my whole life, Lord, be a gift.
Let me know that other men are not strangers, but my
brothers,
    for everything that separates us is a step backward,
    and everything that joins us is a step forward;
    everything that turns me to myself is a halt in my
    growth and an exercise in non-being;
    and everything I give is a step towards fulfilment and
    an exercise in being.

With you watching me, Lord, I will go out to meet others.
I will be the one who asks them to give themselves;
    and thus I will do them the greatest possible service,
    for I will be helping them to become 'the image of
    God'—gods, in your Son Jesus Christ.

18. The dead are alive

I climbed as quickly as I could to the third floor. One of our neighbours had come to fetch me. When I entered the flat, his wife turned towards me. Her face was covered with tears. 'It's over,' she sobbed. 'it's all over.' Her mother had just died.

My husband and I tried to do what we could for our bereaved neighbours. And, yesterday morning, after the funeral, we went to the cemetery with them. My husband had taken the morning off.

Last night, we thanked God for the kindness that everyone in our building had shown our friends. We have come a long way in two years. There was a time when most of the tenants in our building lived in separate little ivory towers. Many of them spoke to their neighbours only to complain or to fight. Now, when we suggested to one couple that they take up a collection for flowers for the funeral, they readily agreed—and this was the same couple who, not too long ago, absolutely refused, under any conditions 'to mind anybody else's business', as they put it. The only way to live in peace, they used to argue, was for everyone to keep to themselves and leave their neighbours alone.

But our prayer was not only a prayer of thanksgiving, for we have discovered some serious shortcomings in our own behaviour.

For example, we could not find the courage to ask the two Christian couples in our building to attend the mass that we had celebrated for our neighbour's mother. And, worse, I didn't speak to my bereaved friend about the

Christian mystery of death. She herself is a Christian, we tried to console her at the purely human level. It was because we were shy, I suppose; but, to be frank, it was also because we lack faith. We've never really thought about the mystery of death; and when it has come into our minds we've been content to talk glibly about the survival of the 'soul'. I think that we were afraid—afraid that if we thought about it too long, we would have to face the poverty and fragility of our own belief.

Now, since death has come so close, the Lord invites us to reflect. We were so struck by this that my husband and I together spent some time going over our attitude towards death.

How often people say:

'What a beautiful life she had . . . ' (an attempt to use the past in order to console), or

'Poor woman! She didn't have a chance to enjoy her retirement . . .' (Is this really the Christian ideal of old age?), or

'At least she died peacefully. She didn't suffer . . .' (a human value).

Like other people, we have spoken of 'the remains', the more or less eternal 'grief'. And we, too, have sighed, 'It's all over.'

These are only words, of course. But words reveal attitudes—and these are the attitudes not of pagans, but of 'de-Christianised Christians'. We have no reason to be proud of them.

And yet, we believe in Jesus Christ, and Jesus tells us today, once more, that for himself and for Christians there is no such thing as death. Death once came into the world because of sin; but Jesus has conquered death. 'I am the resurrection. If anyone believes in me, even though he dies he will live, and whoever lives and believes in me will never die' (*John* 11: 25–26).

'Anyone who follows me will not be walking in the dark; he will have the light of life' (*John* 8: 12).

'Eternal life' is not a life which begins after death. It has its source on earth. Jesus offers 'water' to thirsty mankind, as he offered it to the Samaritan woman; and in him that water will become 'a spring inside him, welling up to eternal life' (*John* 4: 14). Those who live in Christ have already, in him, risen from the dead.

'I tell you most solemnly, everybody who believes has eternal life' (*John* 6: 47).

'Anyone who does eat my flesh and drink my blood has eternal life' (*John* 6: 54).

The whole of creation, including 'matter' and 'bodies' will enter into eternity by virtue of the Redemption. 'The whole creation is eagerly waiting for God to reveal his sons . . . creation still retains the hope of being freed, like us, from its slavery to decadence, to enjoy the same freedom and glory as the children of God. From the beginning till now the entire creation, as we know, has been groaning in one great act of giving birth' (*Rom.* 8: 19–22).

Jesus, by his resurrection, has given an entirely new direction to human progress. Now, an irresistible current draws all those who have been redeemed in the wake of the risen Christ. Death is only a step, the attainment of man's final life where the Lord is waiting for us. 'Do not let your hearts be troubled. Trust in God still, and trust in me. There are many rooms in my Father's house; if there were not, I should have told you. I am going now to prepare a place for you. . . . I shall return to take you with me; so that where I am, you may be too. You know the way to the place where I am going . . . I am the Way, the Truth and the Life' (*John* 14: 1–4, 6).

We must not let our imagination be led astray by the simplicity of Jesus' language. The imagination tends to materialise spiritual realities. We think of heaven as billowing clouds, and the saved as people wearing white robes and carrying harps. But heaven is inconceivable, unimaginable, for it is infinite Love. To be 'in heaven' means to live in the love of the Trinity.

The belief in eternal life is a matter of pure faith, but not of irrational faith. The rhythm of nature, man's deepest aspirations, the universal straining of mankind and of the world towards the spirit—all this constitutes a forward progress, an effort to rise above oneself in order to attain fulfilment beyond the dimension of time.

The seed which falls into the earth is not lost. It germinates, and pours out a richer and more abundant life.

The seed which is eaten does not die. It flourishes in another, fuller, life.

At the purely human level, men do not die either. They live in others—in their children and grandchildren. They live in all those to whom they gave themselves; that is, in all those whom they loved. And they live also, until the end of time, in their actions and in the consequences of their actions.

Every man is an appeal to the dimension of infinity. He must therefore be either an absurdity, an incomprehensible monster, the incredible result of blind chance—either that, or there must be an answer to the question which he embodies.

An engineer designs and builds an automobile with no end in mind other than that it be a means of transportation.

The bird has wings so that it may fly.

Why would man have infinite faculties—reason, consciousness, imagination—if he were not destined to live at the level of infinity?

The discoveries of Teilhard de Chardin (and of many others), with their extraordinary flashes of intuition, describe to us the tendency of mankind and of the universe towards greater consciousness and greater knowledge, the great effort of all life to overcome the limitations of time and to enter the eternal dimension. And Saint-Exupéry tells us that 'The only reason for being on earth is to work at becoming.'

From the human standpoint, we can reasonably believe in the eternal destiny of man and the universe—i.e., in the prodigious growth of the seeds of the infinite which have been planted within them. And revelation confirms and surpasses, by far, what we feel in our minds—for it is not a human life which we are offered, but, in Jesus, a divinised life.

There is no death. The dead are alive, for they are members of the total Body of Christ, as we ourselves are. We are in a spiritual relationship with them. It is true that our senses cannot perceive their bodies; but it is also true that they are no longer subject to corporeal limitations, and we can communicate with them in faith.

Whoever receives Christ in the Eucharist receives his whole Body, for the dead and risen Christ cannot be separated from his brothers. To receive Christ in the Eucharist is to receive 'the living' from beyond—that is, to be in deep communication, in Christ, with the dead.

For a Christian, physical death is not the end. It is a step; an entry into life. For a Christian, there are no 'dear departed'. There are only the living, those living in Christ. Only sin separates, for only sin can bring death.

Lord, I am struck with awe in the presence of this great mystery. Even when I am filled with earthly satisfaction, there comes

> a moment when my body trembles, and I know that my spirit is still unsatisfied.
> But when my spirit and my heart are content, joy fills me completely
> and I sense that this joy goes far beyond the satisfaction of my senses, and that it is akin to infinite joy.

I exist at the relative level, while what I need is the absolute.

I exist at the temporal level, while what I need is the eternal.
I exist at the finite level, while what I need is the infinite.
Lord, I cannot make myself believe
    that I am a fish out of water,
    a bird without a sky,
    a question without an answer,
    a road without an end.

I cannot believe that love is only a chemical reaction and
that it does not survive the last beat of a man's heart.

I cannot believe that the incredible evolution of man and the
universe,
    which goes back to the beginning of time
    and continues today,
        is all in vain.

Lord, I accept your divine revelation
    as the great culmination of creation,
    as the answer of love to my essential question.

It is not a tranquilliser to set my mind at ease,
    and it is not an invitation to escape from the world.
It is instead a reason for me to take root in the earth
    from whence comes *life*.

'Martha said to Jesus: "If you had been here, my brother
would not have died."
'Jesus said: "I am the resurrection.
    If anyone believes in me, even though he dies he will
    live,
    and whoever lives and believes in me
    will never die.
    Do you believe this?"
' "Yes, Lord," she said, "I believe that you are the Christ" '
(*John* 11: 21–27).

19. The age of anguish

I've just finished reading an article on Sweden. It seems to be a country which has succeeded in solving many of its social problems. But it also seems to be an anguished country, a country faced with serious 'moral' problems. Periodically, it seems, young people in Sweden rebel against society with no apparent reason.

A friend of mine has just returned from a visit to the United States. He's told me about his experiences with drug-addicts, hippies and 'communes' of young people all trying desperately to discover the meaning of their lives. He showed me a newspaper he brought back with him. On page one, there was a story about a young man of seventeen who had killed his fourteen-year-old girlfriend. He explained to the police that he 'wanted to see what it was like to kill someone'.

Either directly or indirectly, I know many young people who have tried to kill themselves. Medical men, psychiatrists and psychologists, tell us that the number of suicides among young people is growing at an alarming rate. The answer usually given, when someone asks a young man or woman why they want to kill themselves, is something like this: 'It's just that life isn't worth the trouble of living.'

Over the past months, I have become particularly sensitive to the anguish of man today. I've been listening, reading, observing. The fact of man's essential discontentment with his life and with the world is in evidence everywhere: in the streets, in the offices and factories, in public debates and private conversations, and, of course, in the headlines of the newspapers and magazines.

Our contemporaries, in the midst of suffering and disorder, are looking for a way, a direction for their lives, *a reason for living*. We have entered the Age of Anguish.

It is time for me to stop and ask myself, in the light of faith, what Jesus is telling me by and in man's dissatisfaction.

There are some men who ask no questions. That is very bad, for men who do not ask questions are not really human. None the less, these same men will one day ask: Is there a meaning to my life? And they will not be prepared to answer that question. They will try to forget it, and they will not be able to; for to forget such a question is impossible.

There are some men who settle down in life and forget that life has any purpose other than living. They surround themselves with material goods, and, always greedy for more, they never have enough. They are condemned to a life of perpetual dissatisfaction, for, they no sooner manage to satisfy one desire than ten more rise up to take its place. They are like slaves who work until they drop, and yet have nothing to show for their pains.

Many men—the majority—have experienced human love. They have made a home and had children. This was their immediate goal, and a noble one. Such men live for their homes and their families. But they have not solved *the* problem of their lives; they have only postponed it. One day, a day of suffering or worry, the problem will reappear: why continue to struggle? For the children? But what is the purpose of children? Why have children at all? Indeed, why live?

There are men who believe in the supremacy of technology and science. They are proud of man's intelligence and power, and they believe that these things will create an ideal world capable of satisfying man's deepest aspirations.

None the less, however proud man may be of his victories

over the limits of time, of knowledge and of life, the fact remains that these limits are still there to frustrate and exasperate him.

There are other men who stand in fear before the power of technology and science. They are like children terrified by a great machine which they have somehow set in motion and cannot stop. Will they be able to control this power? How will it be used? And, why?

Some men live by violence. They are fighting against an unknown enemy. All they know is that they must take revenge because they were only given little joys when they were looking for happiness. They were looking for happiness—but what kind of happiness? They are like blind men lost in an unfamiliar street. And these are the men whom we call rebels without a cause.

There are, on the other hand, those who are engaged in a legitimate struggle against society. We try to inundate them with 'consumer goods', but we ignore other desires in them —desires and hungers which grow keener every day. These men therefore try to destroy society by working against its economic, social and political structures. They have plans, projects; but they look vainly about the world for any concrete realisation of the kind of man and the kind of society of which they dream. Where they find signs of clear progress, they also find signs of terrible crises and of the profound dissatisfaction of men.

There are some men today who try to escape from a world which they find either too dull or too gaudy. Having no responsibilities, no creative power and no hope, they are suffocating in a world of asphalt and concrete. Such men have travelled dead-end roads. They have been immobilised by one-way streets, traffic lights and detours. They have therefore fled, and now they follow paths which lead nowhere: eroticism, drugs and false mysticism. They wish to escape, at any price. But escape where? For them, there is no 'elsewhere'.

The essential incompleteness of man, his imperfection, his failure to fulfil himself and to build a new and better world; his anguish over himself, his life and the world; the anguish which underlies his existence, or the anguish which appears everywhere as mankind, in its splendid folly, rushes along the road of progress—all of this anguish is in fact an *unconscious yearning for a God-Saviour, for a God-Love who gives a meaning to all men and all things.*

A man's life and his development, and the life and development of mankind itself, can have only one meaning and one direction: *God-Love.* When man and mankind are deprived of God-Love, they become frustrated and directionless.

When the hub of a wheel is removed, the spokes scatter. In the same way, when the evolution of mankind loses its centre, man is condemned to chaos and despair.

By perpetually increasing our material goods and making them an end in themselves, we make it more and more difficult for ourselves to discover and to follow *God-Love.* This is what Jesus meant when he told us that it is very hard for a rich man to enter the kingdom of heaven.

The most tragic thing that can happen to a man is for him to mistake the means for the end. He then finishes by adoring idols, which become his substitute gods. But they cannot replace the living God.

The true God remains present to all men, but we become less and less capable of seeing him. He is omnipresent; but we make him omni-absent.

Our grandparents were content to think of heaven as being 'up there'. But their picture of it, as the home of fat little angels with haloes walking around in the clouds, has made us forget heaven's true nature. Our contemporaries are right when they refuse to believe that heaven is 'in the sky'. It is not in the sky. It is down at the corner of the street—in a transcendent manner, of course. For the Kingdom of God is already among us.

Our Christianity is a part of history. Our faith is a commitment to that history. The kingdom of heaven has to be built, but 'If Yahweh does not build the house, in vain the masons toil' (Ps. 127: 1).

We are not asked to 'defend the rights of God' by struggling to have his symbols on a wall or on a flag, or his name in a rule or a law. No matter how frightened we may be by the modern world, we must not 'take refuge in God' by means of prayer or pseudo-mysticism. What we must do is to *re-discover God in our lives.* Some people have tried to take God out of life to keep him 'safe'; and some have tried to force him out of it. The majority of men, however, simply do not know that he is there.

God-Love is present to man and to the world,

    as sap is present in a tree,

    as leaven is present in bread,

    as life is present in a body.

It is up to us to meet him, to love him, to struggle at his side in order to free mankind. It is up to us to make his presence known.

We feel sorry for people who do not know why, or for whom, they live. Sometimes we are scandalised by their lack of awareness. But can we truthfully say that, for practical purposes, our own lives are centred round our brothers and round God-Love who is at the heart of our brothers and of the world?

Most of our actions, even our supposedly 'apostolic' actions, are performed without a clear vision of the end at which they are aimed.

The alliance between the Creator and the creature must be realised within ourselves. We must re-discover the Centre: God-Love. We must build within ourselves, but on the 'Rock', the corner stone, which is Jesus Christ. Then, from our present situation on earth as pilings under a structure, we and our brothers will be able to 'build a tower with its top reaching heaven'.

More than ever before, men today have need of a Saviour.

Without knowing it, they are crying out to him. As Christians, we know that this Saviour is our friend, that we are his brothers and that God, his Father, is our Father. If we live as sons and brothers, then men will recognise the Saviour in us.

Lord, tonight, in the quiet darkness, I heard the world heave a deep sigh,
 I heard the tragic cry of anguished men.
They do not know where to turn, and therefore
 they are searching blindly,
 losing themselves, rebelling,
 or simply resigning themselves.

Make me open my ears and my heart so that
 I may be able to hear their cries and discover their meaning.
Give me the strength to gather up these cries
 and offer them to you as one immense supplication
 rising from earth towards you—a prayer:

 Lord, do not forget our alliance.
 Show yourself to us.
 We need you.
 You are our Saviour.

Help me to find you—I, who so often act as though you were not there.
Help me to belong to the world,
 but with you within myself,
 in my heart,
 in my living flesh,
 in my human actions.

Help me to be one of those who walk,
 who walk in life where men walk,

with men,
as a man,
without looking at my feet,
without stumbling as though I were blind,
but with my eyes open, as one who sees.

Then, Lord, perhaps if they see me walking among them,
as a man who sees,
they will be freed from their anguish.

20. We have too much to do

We don't even know where to start. My husband and I are 'involved'. He's active in his union, in a cooperative, and in our community association. I belong to the parent–teachers' association, and I work in my parish as a catechism-teacher and as an officer of various clubs. We have meetings to attend, books to read—and we are constantly being asked to join this or that movement or organisation.

We have our home, of course, and our children. We have relatives, friends, people we know from work, our neighbours. We think that our lives are full; that we are doing enough. Yet, we compare what we are *not* doing with what we are doing, and we see how much there is still to be done. The very magnitude of the task seems to solicit our help, to *demand* it. And still, we must find time to read, to pray, to relax, to sleep. We don't know what to do. There is simply too much to do.

In the midst of this feeling of frustration and of powerlessness, we paused and tried to find out what the Lord was trying to tell us.

First of all, we must learn to accept our frustration. It is possible to reduce it; but we must face the fact that it will exist, no matter what we do, for the rest of our lives. We will *always* be asked to do infinitely more than we are capable of doing.

What we must learn is to face that situation, accept it and offer it to God. This will help to lessen our frustration by lessening its power to discourage and exasperate us. Even more, it enables us to make use of our frustration by converting it into a means of redemption—like the Cross, the scene of the tragic 'frustration' of Jesus Christ as he hung between heaven and earth, between sin and love, between life and death.

We must reconcile ourselves to the fact that we cannot always see things clearly. We sometimes have obligations which seem contradictory, and it is difficult to choose between them. We would like to have a straight road, but in fact it has many forks. It is only by going forward that we will find signposts, that we will discover whether to turn off or go straight on, whether to take the right or the left turning. In other words, we must learn to live in faith. We must sharpen our sight in order to be able to read the wishes of the Father in what happens around us. We must learn to trust him and to let him be our guide through the maze of roads that lie ahead. We must learn to let ourselves be led at the very moment that we wish to go our own way.

We must learn to accept our limitations, however humiliating, exasperating and crippling they may be. These are the limitations imposed by time, our strength and our health, our material means, our intelligence, the people with whom we work and the thousand other things which prevent us from doing as much as we would like. These limitations are felt all the more keenly as our mind is quick to conceive, our heart quick to be moved, our ears quick to hear the cries of our brothers; for then they make us painfully aware of the chasm separating reality from possibility. We must acknowledge that

> we are doing only one-tenth of what we can clearly see we should be doing;
> we are doing only one-hundredth of what we could do, if only. . . .
> we are doing only one-thousandth of what we would like to do. . . .

In an active life, the hardest thing by far is to accept one's limitations. We must not forget that the Cross was not very large, and that the drama of crucifixion did not require much time or many words. Yet, it was sufficient to hold much suffering, and the infinity of love.

To act—in the sense of participating—means to struggle constantly against selfishness; and to become less selfish we require the cross. There can be no conscious act on earth that does not have need of being redeemed. The bond between action and redemption is one that has been created by sin.

If we are to succeed in our work, we must learn to offer to God the frustrations of our apostolic lives, the problems in discovering our duty, and the burdens of our limitations. This is the *sine qua non* of successful action.

Frustration, therefore, is inevitable in our lives. But it can be greatly reduced, and *it should never deprive us of interior peace*. Everything depends upon our faith and our love.

We are not expected to do everything by ourselves. We have the time and the means to do what the Father wants us to do. Therefore, if we do not have the time or the means to do something, we may conclude that the Father does not expect us to do it. So why should we become discouraged or disgusted?

We should be humble enough to know that we are not indispensable at any given moment, in any given situation, to any given person. We must be very strict in judging the authenticity of our motives for commitment. Sometimes we are not motivated by the desire to serve our brothers but, unconsciously, by pride, aggressiveness, the wish for power or simply by a desire to escape from a humdrum life or an unpleasant home situation.

What is most important is not the sum total of what we do, but *the intensity of the love which transforms our actions*.

Plasma enters and gives life to the body of a sick man through a tiny hole in a needle. In the same way, an authentic commitment, undertaken in love, benefits the whole of mankind, no matter where the love is lived and no matter what the human dimension of that commitment.

Through our action, however limited, we participate in mankind's universal progress. If we act with Jesus Christ, through him we are building the Kingdom of the Father.

If we are exhausted by the many things we have to do, if we dissipate our energies and become discouraged, it is because we forget the basic unity among all things. We are looking up at the sky, and we see only the branches of the tree. But, if we lower our eyes and look closely, we will see the trunk which feeds all the branches with its sap.

Too often, we go from branch to branch and forget about the trunk.

'I am the vine, you are the branches. Whoever remains in me, with me in him, bears fruit in plenty; for cut off from me you can do nothing. Anyone who does not remain in me is like a branch that has been thrown away—he withers; these branches are collected and thrown on the fire, and they are burned' (*John* 15: 5–6).

The more numerous our commitments, the more diverse our work, the more time-consuming our participation, then the more we should stop and contemplate the only source of all action, Jesus Christ. In his light, we will discover, and learn to live, the basic unity of what we do.

If the diversity of our commitments disturbs us, it is because we do not throw ourselves entirely into each of them. We cannot, because we are fragmented:

a part of us dreams about what should be done;
a part is busy worrying about a particular event or person;
a part remains attached to the past;
and a part is speculating on the future.

If we knew how to concentrate, we would be able to do more things in less time, and we would do them much more efficiently.

What harms us and exhausts us is this practice of living our lives 'in pieces'. When we can truly say, with St Paul, that we are 'all things to all men', then we will have peace and joy.

We must give all of our attention and all our strength to each one of our actions; for each of our actions is for us, and for the moment, *the only thing that God wants us to do*.

Only Jesus Christ can give us interior unity. And only he can unify our apostolic lives in the midst of our commitments. *There is only one love to be lived* through the demands made upon us by our brothers.

Lord, here we are,
    out of breath,
    out of courage,
    and almost out of hope.
Caught between the infinity of our desires
    and the limitations of our means,
        we're tossed about,
        torn,
        pulled here and pulled there,
        confused,
        and exhausted.
So, Lord, here we are,
    finally still,
    and finally ready to listen.

You've seen how our dissatisfaction has made us suffer.
You've seen how fear has led us astray in choosing our commitments.
You've seen how we were afraid of doing too little.
And you've seen the cross imposed by our limited means.

Lord, make us strong enough to do what we should do,
    calmly,
    simply,

without wanting to do too much,
without wanting to do it all ourselves.
In other words, Lord, make us humble
in our wish and our will to serve.
Help us above all to find you in our commitments,
For you are the unity of our actions;
You are the single love
in all our loves,
in all our efforts.

You are the well spring,
And all things are drawn to you.
So, we have come before you, Lord,
to rest and gather our strength.

21. It's Christmas at our house

We are happy because we have a son. His name is Benedict, and he was born yesterday—a healthy eight-pound boy. We wanted a son with all our hearts and, with God, we created him. My wife is still in the hospital. I visited her today, and we took a moment to reflect together on the great mystery of life and on our own joy so as to give it an eternal dimension. But it has not all been joyful. We have also shared the difficulties, anguish and failings common to man who is so often unaware, selfish and weak with respect to his extraordinary creative power.

This evening, I had a talk with our parish priest, and then I had dinner with my brother and sister-in-law (our two other children are staying with them). I went home immediately after eating, and our house seemed empty and lifeless. I wandered around like a 'lost soul', missing something: the tangible affection of the woman who has become 'one' with me. Yet, I am bound to her by love now, just as I was a few hours ago when I embraced her at the hospital. And I know that these reflections are hers as well as my own.

My wife and I, before reflecting on the grandeur of our mission as human beings, and before speaking of our happiness at the birth of our son, recalled first of all the reactions of our friends and acquaintances at the news of my wife's pregnancy.

These reactions fall into several categories. There was the unbounded and healthy joy registered by young couples who want children themselves. Then there was the quiet acceptance of older couples who, with children of their own, are quite aware of the efforts and sacrifices entailed in raising a family. And finally, there was the look of horror upon the faces of those who regarded another child as nothing short of a catastrophe.

When my wife told a friend of hers that she was pregnant, the friend immediately tried to console and encourage her. Pregnancy, she felt, was a difficult burden; but since it had happened, it had to be accepted. Some of the people in our neighbourhood are not so willing to resign themselves to the inevitable. My wife has heard older, more 'experienced' women giving advice on how to terminate pregnancy and handing over the addresses of certain persons who know how to handle such things.

At work, some of my friends congratulated me, and I know that they were sincere. Others, however, either in whispers or aloud, behind my back or to my face, made fun of me or joked about my wife's pregnancy: 'You obviously don't know what to do,' and 'You let your wife put one over on you.' In any case, their comments usually provided an opening for a hundred obscene jokes and locker-room stories, some of them supposedly based on 'personal experience'.

My wife and I did not try to change our attitude towards these people, but to understand their general problem and the particular problems of each individual. Then we tried to meditate, in faith, on the exciting but frightening mystery of life. Alone, we certainly cannot find practical solutions to home and family problems. We know that there are no ready-made solutions, and that there are no solutions which fit every case in every circumstance. None the less, we tried very hard to keep in mind both aspects of the problem: first, the enormous difficulty of living, in love, the mystery of creation; and, second, the infinite grandeur of that mystery.

God is, above all, the great Master of life. He teaches us

that life is sacred: 'Every hair on your head has been counted' (*Matt.* 10: 30).

God is the source of life, and life flourishes in Jesus Christ: '. . . for in him were created all things in heaven and on earth; everything visible and everything invisible . . . all things were created through him and for him' (*Col.* 1: 16).

It is God's will that man participate, on his own responsibility, in the creation of other men. But creation is the result of love, and therefore man can truly create only out of authentic love. A man who is not created in love is 'badly' created.

Parents who take on the responsibility of giving life to a child, simultaneously take on the responsibility of developing that life. To rear a child is to continue to create that child. And, since all creation requires love, children who are loved inadequately are 'ill bred'.

A man who creates is truly the image of the God-Creator. The family unit—father, mother, child—is a living reflection of the Trinity. To create a human being means to give a brother to other men. For a Christian, it also means to give a brother to Jesus and a son to the Father in heaven. The greatest and noblest power given to man, therefore, is that of having children. But this can be hard to believe in view of how often we are petty, weak and even vicious, with respect to that power.

God gave the earth to man so that man could rule it and complete it. Nature in general is still in a state of savagery; and that particular part of nature which is the human body is in the same state. The body, therefore, along with all its faculties, must be humanised and personalised. This involves the long and difficult work of integrating all of man's energies in the unity of the person.

Human sexuality, since it influences man at every level of his being, must also be integrated. Even more, it must be permeated with love in order to carry out fully and at every level its role as the source of life. Husband and wife, in giving themselves to one another, are giving life to each other. They re-create themselves before giving life together to a third human being.

This integration of human sexuality is not easy. Man's impulses and instincts do not willingly obey his mind. And human selfishness tends to separate sexual pleasure from its mission of union in love and from its creative role, making of it an end in itself.

Mature, self-sufficient human beings who have decent homes should be free to have as many children as they want. Every birth should be the result of a truly human decision, and not the consequence of hit-or-miss calculations, or of a moment of weakness with respect to a poorly kept resolution, or of ineffective 'precautions', or of a simple 'mistake'. A man and wife should freely decide, before God, the number of children that they can decently support, and then *they should control pregnancy in accordance with that decision.*[1]

There is a great discrepancy between the ideal and the real, between the grandeur of our vocation as co-creators and the often painful and disappointing realisation of that vocation. We must accept our situation as both human beings and sinners.

A family, like a man, is not ready-made. It has to be built up. There is no such thing as a perfect family. There are only families making progress towards their proper proportions and towards their creative unity. A Christian knows that the sacrament of matrimony channels the whole love of Christ the Saviour into human love, and that this saving love saves and transforms human love. This is the hope and the strength of human love.

There is evil outside ourselves, in our environment, in the world. Here again, it is human selfishness that makes evil exist and grow and allows it to affect our cities, our suburbs,

1. So far as the *means* of control are concerned, this is a serious problem and one which is beyond the scope of this book.

our work, our laws and all our structures in one way or another: poor health, resulting from ecological imbalances created by our way of life; inadequate and unhealthy housing which makes it impossible for families to grow; salaries which are insufficient to support a family; working conditions which endanger pregnancy and sometimes result in spontaneous abortion. We might also cite the marks of underdevelopment which afflict the world: hunger, slums, illiteracy, disease, unemployment and so forth. These things kill children by the millions and prevent the birth of others who would otherwise have come into the world.

If we were to compile a partial list of man's sins against creation, it would read something like this: the lack of self-mastery which prevents a man from integrating and harmonising all his faculties; human selfishness, which uses man's unifying and creative power for ends other than those for which they were intended; a world so poorly organised that it does not allow mankind to develop in a healthy manner.

If we are to abolish these abuses, we must work with all our strength so that: available land, which is capable of feeding all of mankind, may be better distributed and more effectively cultivated; science and technology may be used for man's good, so as to solve the problems of hunger, housing, etc.; medical research and psychology may discover an effective and dependable means of controlling births; man may take steps to realise his interior unity by integrating and personalising all his faculties, that he may fight against the spirit of selfishness and develop authentic love, and, above all, that he may learn to motivate and understand the meaning of his struggle by attaining to a clear vision of the extraordinary mission confided to him by God, and that he may encounter Jesus Christ in order to accomplish that mission with him.

I wrote the following prayer for my wife and me to recite tomorrow. We will do so, thinking of ourselves, our brothers, the child God has given us, and especially of those who are born outside of love.

Lord, here is your son, Benedict.
> He is your son as well as ours.
> We have created him together, in love;
> and, if you will help us,
> together we will make him grow in love.

Lord, we are a father and mother,
> indissolubly united in this new life which is the marvellous result of our love made flesh.

We are closer to you than we were, because with you we have created.
> Thank you for having made us so great.

Although you are the almighty Creator,
> you needed us to create a human being.
> You needed us, Father, to give you a new son.
> You needed us, Jesus, to give you a new brother.
> Thank you for having made us so great.

This child is the Father's plan of love which,
> through human love,
> has once more been made flesh.

This child has been invited
> to know the eternal love of the Trinity.

This child,
> because he is a human being,
> because he is a member of your ever-growing total Body,
> —this child is you, Lord:

'Listen, I bring you news of great joy, a joy to be shared by the whole people . . . a saviour has been born to you; he is Christ the Lord.'
> Lord, it's Christmas at our house.

Forgive us, Lord, for not being overjoyed at this great mystery.

Forgive us for being too happy for ourselves, and not happy enough for you and for him.

Forgive us, above all, for all the children whom their parents have 'by mistake'.

Forgive us for all the children that selfish and misguided people refuse to have.

And forgive us for this badly organised world which mutilates your Body.

You must understand, Lord, that we are only men
    and that we are prisoners of the flesh.
    We're not yet used to living like gods.
    Help us, Lord.
You know that this great hunger we feel within ourselves, in our hearts, even though we pervert it and try to ignore it, is really an overwhelming desire to live the great mystery of Unity and of Creation.
        You know it Lord. But we don't.

We wanted a son, with all our strength and all our love.

But we understand the searching, the struggles, the failures and the despair of others.

We know that tomorrow it will be our turn to reflect, to take our places on the battlements, and to fight.

Keep us from being proud and too sure of ourselves.

Lord, you see mankind with its great problems, its defeats and its victories.

Preserve man from solutions that would destroy him.
    Give him respect for life,
        love of life;
            For you, Father, are life itself.

22. The Christian in action

What is the value of my actions compared to the incredible amount of work that must be done in the world? This question first came to my mind a few days ago. I don't recall what happened to make me think of it. Since then, the idea has preoccupied me. It sits on my conscience like an undigested meal sitting on my stomach. And, like a corrosive acid, it has gradually affected the whole of me, down to the roots of my being. Now, I'm dissatisfied, disturbed, discouraged. A single conclusion seems inescapable: I am accomplishing absolutely nothing.

I see the world around me with its enormous problems. If I need to be reminded of those problems, I have only to look at the newspapers. They are full of them. Hundreds of millions of human beings do not have enough to eat. They live in miserable slums. They are illiterate. And they are exploited by their brothers. Whole nations, unable to bear their suffering any longer, are awakening and beginning to stir. And a few generous souls, and a few madmen, are appearing, beginning to organise and to fight. But they are usually crushed by the forces of 'law and order'. And here I am, so proud of being a 'militant'. I'm nothing more than a child. I worry about painting a room while the whole house is falling down around me. I weed my garden while the city is going up in flames. What can I say?—except that I am accomplishing absolutely nothing.

I was wrong not to stop and think of this sooner. And I was especially wrong not to talk about it with my friends. I've now discovered that some of them also have many doubts—for other reasons—about the real value of what they are doing.

This evening, a few of my friends and I went to talk to our parish priest. Here is what I've retained of that session.

I discovered, first of all, that my doubts about the value of my work were nothing more than a subtle temptation to stop working. The temptation, if I do not overcome it, will weaken me to the point that, one day, I will simply decide to sit down and relax instead of continuing to move forward.

I also realised that, at the purely temporal level, I did not have a sufficient understanding of the collective and international aspects of the problems of humanity. I found out, too, that for me to be able to do something about injustices perpetrated far from where I live and work, it is enough for me to be committed where I am.

Why do we always want to be doing something other than what we are able to do and supposed to be doing? Why do we always want to go somewhere else, in the belief that we could do much better there than where we are? So far as I am concerned personally, I can say it is because of an over-active imagination inspired by a hint of good intentions. It is easy to dream, and fun to do so. Too often, I let my mind wander wherever it will. I ignore reality. Meanwhile, life goes on and passes me by without my having been able to influence it and especially without my having illuminated it with the light of love.

I was quite right in saying that often I accomplish absolutely nothing. I do nothing when I waste my time, my life and my love in dreaming about the things I *could* do, while ignoring the things that I *should* do. I am like a man in an assembly line who ignores his work and slows down the whole process of production.

The most important consequence of our meeting with our parish priest has been that I've re-examined my attitude in light of faith, and also at the level of content.

So far as the light of faith is concerned, it enables me to act in conjunction with Someone who has invited me to do so; Someone who, before me, was fighting to save mankind. I must work with him. I know this, of course; but I often forget it.

At the level of the content of my action, I spend too much time working for an entirely superficial liberation of mankind—sometimes even for a liberation which has nothing to do with man himself.[1] I should be working for his *total* liberation; that is, for his freedom in his innermost being, where life has its origin and where, simultaneously and mysteriously, selfishness also has its origin—that selfishness which serves to alienate man from himself. At that level, only the salvation conferred by Jesus Christ can be effective.

It is true that the liberation of man takes place at different levels, and that all aspects of it are not alike. But it is equally true that liberation is accomplished by a single movement and a single struggle. For everything is bound together in the unity of a single person and a single humanity.

In that sense, it would be absurd to believe that if we struggle for the economic, social and political liberation of our brothers, there must automatically be a change of heart in those who are struggling and in those on behalf of whom the struggle is being carried forward. The fact is that a battle may be spoiled. Often, it must be not only purified, but also *saved*. Commitment can be carried to its most effective conclusion only if it is *a result of love and a carrier of love*. And, for a Christian, it can be effective only if it is consciously lived in Christ the Saviour and with him.

It would be equally absurd to believe that man can be truly freed from his selfishness if he is not committed to the struggle for his own total liberation and that of his

1. I do not mean to imply that any aspect of life or any structure is without consequence for man; for things which often seem extremely remote may be links in the chains which hold mankind prisoner. These chains are longer than we think.

brothers. This commitment is the only and absolute criterion of the presence of redemptive love. We can only be saved by becoming saviours.

Thus, when I have doubts about the value of my insignificant and limited work, it is because I see only one aspect of it: its tangible, visible aspect. This aspect is real, but it is not the whole of reality.

I believe in working for justice and human dignity. I believe in demonstrations, meetings, motions and petitions. I believe in pamphlets, posters and votes. I believe in unions and political parties. I am willing to become involved in an extended and difficult struggle. But, I hesitate to stop and reappraise my commitment in the light of love. I am reluctant to spend fifteen minutes talking to the One who, in the midst of the battle and in a 'beyond' which we can see only in the light of faith, is fighting for the *total liberation* of man. The reason is that I do not believe enough in the power of the planted seed, in that of the leaven in a loaf of bread, or in that of love planted in the earth by the heart of divinised man. I am concerned about perfecting our technological means, but I have forgotten about love.

I sometimes wonder what would happen to the world if we lost control of atomic energy. I visualise a chain reaction, starting from a tiny almost imperceptible space and spreading until it envelops the whole of creation. But it seldom occurs to me to think of the tragic power of a small act of selfishness, a single act which spreads throughout mankind as it does its work of devitalising the total Body of Christ. And it seldom occurs to me to think of the power of a small act of pure love, a single act, which opens the road to new blood in that Body, and which rebuilds its tissues by carrying life to the Body's most distant members. Rarely, too, do I now remember that my human actions, while they must be as well thought out as possible, as serious and as effective as possible, must also be nourished by that *redeeming love*.

You are the only one, Lord, who can teach me apostolic patience. You are the one who, at a particular moment in time and in a particular place, wished to become part of mankind in order to make it free and to make it into your Body. You have channelled the whole of God's eternal Love into the tiny *yes* of an instant's duration. 'Father, if it is possible, let this cup pass me by ... your will be done.' And with your last breath, you said: 'Father, into your hands I commit my spirit.'

Give me the strength not to run away. It takes only one place, one instant, one single act. It will be enough for me to be there, working where you want me to work, in order to save all of mankind. So long as I am willing to welcome redeeming Love, *there is no limit in space or in depth to what I can accomplish.*

Lord, forgive me for working alone.
> When I work alone
>> I see only the face of a man,
>>> a piece of a man.
> I cut man off from what he really is within himself.

Lord, forgive me for working alone.
> When I work alone
>> I reduce my productivity,
>> I devalue it,
>> I deprive it of its revolutionary power
>>> —of the power which,
>> through and beyond mankind's oppressive struc-
>> tures, reaches the heart of man and frees it from
>> slavery.

Lord, forgive me for working alone.
> When I work alone
>> I gradually and inexorably,
>> de-Christianise my work.

Tonight, I come to you once more
    with my life
    and my problems.
    Help me to be entirely present,
        honest, scrupulous, lucid and competent
      in my struggle,
No matter where,
    no matter what the circumstances.
So long as I am doing what you want me to do,
Then, with you, I will save the world
    —the heart of the world;
And, in saving the heart of the world,
      I will save the heart of man.

23. My parents are divorced

My parents are divorced. We are living with mother. She raised us, and it was not an easy job. I resent my father's absence; and yet, I miss him terribly.

I've often thought about him, even though I have only a vague recollection of what he was like. Sometimes, I imagined myself running up to him and spitting in his face out of hatred and contempt. And sometimes, I imagined myself held in his arms and overcome with a love that I thought I had lost for ever. There were times when I cried; but no one knows about that.

I went through a phase when I wanted to root out any memory of him and thus find peace through indifference. I was successful—for a short time; then I was once more overwhelmed by questions, desires and dreams of what could have been. I suffered a great deal; and I translated my suffering into aggression and into a desire for revenge against my mother, against 'everyone', against society and against myself. Finally, exhausted and hurt, I told a priest about my suffering, and we examined it together. I am not free of it now, but it has lost some of its strength. And, above all, it has been transformed into something constructive. *It is my strength*. From now on, I will use it to build, and not to destroy.

Generally speaking, suffering should be met straight-forwardly. To deny suffering is not to abolish it, and to suppress it does not make it disappear. Suffering does not vanish unless the cause of suffering vanishes. Human ways

133

of defending oneself against suffering are only illusions. Even when one manages to 'forget' suffering, it continues to exist internally and to gnaw away at a man until it is recognised for what it is, taken in hand, and *used*.

We do not enjoy suffering, but we ourselves add to it. We harm ourselves, like a traveller who encounters a large rock on his road and throws himself against it again and again until he is wounded and bleeding—and then begins again. Such a man simply refuses to acknowledge that the rock is there.

So long as we do not admit that suffering exists within us and that, in all probability, it will continue to exist, we can never make use of suffering. It is not a matter of resigning ourselves, for that would be like sitting down and refusing to fight. It is rather a question of acknowledging the existence of suffering, integrating it, and transforming it.

My suffering over my father is the more painful because I rebel against it. But it is also more painful because I refuse to face reality. I idealise my father because I don't know him. I know how miserable I've been because he does not live with us; but I have no way of knowing the problems that we would have if he were still living with us.

I've told myself, 'I don't know, and I will never know, a father's love.' And I conclude: 'So, I'm not whole, and I never will be.' But there are two ways to know a parent's love. One way is positive: to experience that love and to live it. The other way is negative: to experience the pain of being deprived of it. The dimension of that pain is exactly proportionate, in depth, to the dimenson and depth of the love that is not known.

I have suffered because a child is his father and mother in one flesh. It's impossible to separate in him what comes from his father and what comes from his mother. In a family, anything which divides husband and wife is indelibly registered in the child's heart. If the parents separate, the child, whether he knows it or not, is torn apart within

134

himself. He becomes a 'split' child; a child divided in his innermost being. Divorce, therefore, is necessarily and always against nature.

A child, since he is his father and his mother in one flesh, is and remains an unbreakable link which binds them together—regardless of their individual situations, and regardless of their relations past, present or future. The child is the permanent witness to the love which once united them. He is their love made flesh. He is their love in a form which cannot be destroyed.

Therefore, even though my parents have spoiled their marriage, if I can grow, evolve, develop; if I can really succeed with my life, then, perhaps without anyone knowing it—not even my parents—*I can save their love.*

In a sense, a child begets his parents. He carries them within himself; and by his life, if he wills to live, and by his love, if he wills to love, *he gives them life.*

I used to ask myself: 'What if I was not really wanted? What if I was only "an accident"?' But then I thought: 'What about those others—those whose parents, or whose fathers, were unknown? What about those who were born as the result of rape, criminal or otherwise?'

What I did not realise was that, even in the most utterly selfish desire, there is always a spark of love. It may be a love which has been repressed, silenced, twisted, deformed and made almost unrecognisable. *But it is still love.* A child is the painful reminder of that hidden love, of that seed of love which wants to germinate. In the child, the parents are for ever united. It may be that love was never *visible* in their relationship. But, if it did not exist before that relationship, it none the less exists after it, in the person of the child.

As a child, I often said: 'I don't love anybody!' I was wrong, of course. If I hadn't loved anyone, I would not have suffered as I did. My suffering was a sign of hidden love.

Since my will to love is unemployed, why not make use

of it? If I repress it, it will deteriorate and turn into something unnatural—into aggression, dissatisfaction, and daydreams. If I make use of it, it will give new life to those around me—to those who, either in the same way or in a different way, have also been deprived of love.

I am alive. I am the result of love, even though it may have been a deformed love. God was part of that love, for there can be no love unless the Father is present. And, because sin was also there, Christ is present. There can be no sin without Christ being there to redeem it.

My suffering is a source of extraordinary strength, and I must make use of it. It was through suffering, *transformed by love*, that Jesus saved the world. Redemption is love in the midst of suffering. If I acknowledge the existence of suffering, if I make use of it, if I nourish it with love— that is, with Jesus Christ—I will save the love spoiled by my parents, and the love spoiled by many others as well.

I must love, and love still more.

I can do anything if I love with Jesus Christ.

Lord, I'm here before you
    because I can't bear to suffer any more.
    I've tried everything:
        to destroy my suffering,
        to forget it,
        to escape from it.

Lord, I'm putting down my burden here, before you.
    I can't carry it another step.
        I've borne it as far as I can,
        I've suffered as much as I can.
Now, I'm turning it over to you, as a friend.

Lord, my arms are empty now.
    I've put down my burden.
    I've given it to you,

After so many days and so many years
 of carrying it tightly in my arms.

I know that the pain continues to live in me,
 and that it will never die.
I am willing to be a child
 torn in two,
 split into pieces
 and bleeding.
 For now I know who I am, Lord.

I am the place where they met.
I am the indissoluble link that bonds them together.
I am the flesh that cannot be destroyed.
I am their love, which lives so long as I live.
I am they, united for ever in marriage.

Lord, I want to live, so that they may live;
 to grow, so that they may grow;
 to love, so that they may love.
And, in silence, I will beget my parents,
 I will give them life,
 I will help them to grow.
I will save them, in saving their love.

24. The rediscovery of nature

Recently, at a meeting of a militant Christian organisation, a woman mentioned that she was involved in a movement to fight against pollution, and that she was gathering signatures locally, for a petition. Some of those present smiled and made remarks about 'fashionable crusades'. But, when we stopped to reflect on what she had said, it became obvious that the anti-pollution movement is a healthy manifestation of opposition to a very real danger.

We didn't have to look very far to find signs of interest in nature all around us. We were astonished at the things that were mentioned in this respect—weekends in the country; a 'return to nature' by people on vacation; the enormous increase in the number of summer houses in the country, in the mountains and at the seaside. And, of course, there are constant campaigns against air-pollution and water-pollution; movements aimed at preserving natural parks and open spaces and at controlling urban sprawl; meetings, congresses and seminars on the preservation of the environment; and the first World Conference on the Environment, convened at Stockholm.[1]

Why this sudden interest in ecology? How does the environment affect man? How does it involve God?

We reflected, and we prayed.

*

1. The conference took place in June 1972, under the sponsorship of the United Nations. More than 1,200 delegates from 179 nations met to study the means of saving our planet.

Man is a social animal. Left to himself, he is incomplete; and, left entirely to himself, he cannot survive. He contains many different elements within himself. He has various faculties which he must unify. He is a member of an enormous group: mankind. He is a cell in an immense body: the universe. He is the son of a Father unique to his many children: God.

If, at one level or another, the links uniting those elements are broken, the result is imbalance, disorder, and, finally, *the mutilation of man*.

In order to be able to live, a man has need of all his physical, emotional and spiritual faculties. But if his sexual or emotional faculties are not integrated into his personality, then these links are broken, and a man is unbalanced because he is incomplete. He is unable to live fully.

Man is made to live in society. He cannot truly grow and live except in relationship to other men. Alone, he must remain underdeveloped and incomplete. In order for him to reach his full growth, he must enter into communication with all men. And, if these links with other men are broken, man is cut off, isolated.

The universe is an extension of man's body. The human body is a piece of earth. Man, in order to live, has need of the earth, the air, the sun—the entire universe. He is necessarily linked to these things. If the links are broken, man is isolated.

Man does not spring from nothingness. He is the fruit of the Father's eternal love. He is a son of the divine household. If he does not recognise his Father, his brother Jesus Christ, and his brothers in Jesus Christ; if he is not freely bound to them and does not live the divine life which is his right as a son, he remains seriously incomplete. In such a case, the bonds have been cut—and the cutting of these bonds is a sin.

This unity of man within himself,
      of men among themselves,
      of men and the universe,

and of all mankind and the whole universe
with the Father in Christ,
constitutes the infinite plan of God which is intended to join
together all things, forever, in the unity of the Trinity.

Whenever man struggles, at one level or another, to
splice together these bonds in love (that is, in freedom, justice and respect for individual and collective values; for
we are talking about a special kind of unity), he is acting in
accordance with God's wish. As a Christian, he must be
committed along with Jesus, who is himself committed to
the unity of the world *at every level*.

In this sense, man's ties to the universe are one aspect,
but a necessary aspect, of his inner equilibrium and of the
world's progress towards unity. It is this aspect with which we
are specially concerned. For, in many cases, these ties have
been loosened, or broken; and, as always happens, disorder
has followed the break and it is destroying the world.

From the beginning, the universe was given to man as a
means of nourishment and growth. It is man's duty to
dominate the universe, develop it and place it at the service
of himself and of all men.

Some men have taken common natural resources and used
them for themselves, to the exclusion of other men. They
have exploited these resources and capitalised on them.

Some men have more water than they need, while others
have not enough. (In the underdeveloped countries, thousands of children die every year because of insufficient water.
And even in the developed countries, there is a serious
injustice in the distribution of water in some of the older
cities.)

The air that some men breathe is pure, while that breathed
by others is polluted.

Some men bask in the sun, while others live in houses
where the sun never enters.

Some men live in the midst of green, open spaces; and
others are surrounded by asphalt and concrete.

Some men build up great holdings of rich land, while other men have no land on which to grow food.

Man has not only made selfish use of the earth for the happiness and pleasure of a few, and condemned others to sickness and early death; he has also exploited the earth without respecting it.

A man who makes use of his body selfishly, for his own pleasure and without reference to any law or measure, disturbs the equilibrium of life; and his weakened body then alienates his spirit. But the earth is an extension of man's body, and when it is not used in accordance with reason, it, too, is stricken with a contagious disease. Today, the earth is diseased. It has been infected by man. The water and the air are polluted, the land is exhausted, and our natural resources have been plundered.[1]

The first ones to suffer, as usual, have been the poor. Weakened by privation, many of them die before their time: factory workers who breathe poisonous fumes for years; children deprived of the sunlight; miners working in darkness.[2] But now pollution is no longer confined to the slums and ghettoes, those concentration camps of human misery. It has begun to spread, to reach the affluent suburbs, to affect commercial interests, to inconvenience the habitués of exclusive resorts. And so, it is attracting a great deal of attention.

1. Magazines and newspapers contain startling figures on this subject. Half the water in the Seine, for example, comes from the sewers of Paris. Mankind burns annually 4·5 billion tons of coal and discharges 100 million tons of carbon dioxide into the atmosphere. Even more striking is the fact that a four-engine jet flying from New York to Paris uses the equivalent of 40 tons of oil and 90 tons of oxygen—i.e., the total amount of oxygen produced daily by 7,500 acres of forest.

2. This is not a bit of demagogic rhetoric or an alarmist's complaint. Statistics reveal a shocking discrepancy in the average longevity of men according to occupation and social class. Literally millions die prematurely from the effects of pollution—the pollution of those very resources which should have enabled them to feed themselves and to develop.

It is not a question of 'halting progress', of depriving of goods those who are already under-consumers. It is not a matter of going backward. But it is a question of controlling and guiding progress in such a way that it will work for the overall good of man and of all men. This is God's first law, given at the beginning of the world. To violate that law is a sin.

It is easy enough to put the blame on others for what is happening to the world's resources. The fact is, however, that we are all polluters of nature. Together, we must share the blame for the world's sickness; and each of us must try to do something about it. For example, we know what exhaust fumes from motor vehicles do to the air, especially in cities. Are we willing to give up the use of our private cars in cities and make use of public transport instead?

We must re-establish the relations with nature that we have broken off. Some people have never reconciled themselves to nature, and we must teach them to do so. Children must make nature's acquaintance and discover the joy of being part of the world. This is the role of a liberal and balanced education.

Everything that works towards a healthy contact between man and nature also works towards man's development, and thus fulfils God's plan for him and for the world.

But we must go still further. We must defend nature from its enemies. This is a duty which God has entrusted to us. We must make use of our bodies—which are a part of this planet—to guide nature, to master it, to humanise it, to make it serve man until it is time for the resurrection.

A commitment to nature (I mean a commitment to respect nature, to achieve an ecological equilibrium, and to develop nature and man's links with it) is not one which is reserved exclusively for sensitive little old ladies with nothing else to do. Certainly, there is a hierarchy of values to be observed in one's commitments; but a commitment to nature, when viewed within the greater context of man's

responsibilities to himself, to society and to the world,
becomes a necessary part of the progress of man and the
universe towards the final harmony of Eternal Love.

Lord, thank you for letting me find my friend who was lost:
    my friend, the earth.
The earth, after all, is made up of the same stuff as I,
    and it needs the light and warmth of the same sun.

We had lost touch with each other for a time.
I no longer saw,
    or visited,
        or even spoke to my friend.
I thought,
    or rather we thought, my brothers and I,
    that we no longer had need of the earth.

Lord, we have found our friend again, but it is sick,
    wounded, and exhausted.
You gave it to us once, and we took it into our hands
    when it was unspoiled,
    savage,
    but able to be tamed.
Some of us betrayed it to the 'developers'
    who forced it to prostitute itself,
    so that they might take their unbridled pleasure from it.
And now, disfigured and contaminated,
    the earth sickens us when we draw near.

Lord, the earth has no arms,
    it has no voice.
Let me be its defender.
Let me fight on its behalf.
For it was you who gave me the earth, Lord;
    you gave it to me and to all men.

In protecting it
    and developing it as you wish,
Once more I will save it,
    and, in saving it,
      save all my brothers.